Consciousness Beyond Death

Consciousness Beyond Death

*New & Old Light
on the Near-Death
Experience*

MICHAEL TYMN

WHITE CROW

www.whitecrowbooks.com

For information: e-mail info@whitecrowbooks.com

Cover Design by Astrid@Astridpaints.com
Interior design by Velin@Perseus-Design.com

Paperback: ISBN: 9781786772831
eBook: ISBN: 9781786772848

Non-Fiction / BODY, MIND & SPIRIT / Psychic
Phenomena / Near-Death Experience

www.whitecrowbooks.com

"The dying experience is almost identical to the experience at birth. It is a birth into a different existence which can be proven quite simply. For thousands of years you were made to "believe" in the things concerning the beyond. But for me, it is no longer a matter of belief, but matter a rather of knowing."

– Elizabeth Kűbler-Ross, M.D.

"I have listened to thousands of people tell their stories of 'going to the other side,' and I can tell you that I believe what they say, and can tell you that for most of them, nothing stands in the way of their faith that another world awaits them."

– Raymond Moody, M.D.

"This [near-death] experience gave me a feeling of extreme poverty, but at the same time of great fullness. There was no longer anything I wanted or desired. I existed in an objective form; I was what I had been and lived."

– C. G. Jung, M.D.

Contents

Preface: New and Old Light on the NDE. 1

1. Taking Your Toys with You at Death 7

2. NDE Researcher Sees Life as a Paradox 13

3. Overwhelming Evidence for the Survival of
Consciousness 19

4. Experiencing a Pre-Death Life Review 27

5. Dealing with Doubting Thomas Syndrome 33

6. Admiral Tells of Drowning and What Happened After. . .43

7. The Most Profound NDE ever? 51

8. The Physician Who Watched Himself Die 57

9. Sort of a Cloud but Not a Cloud 63

10. The Most Dynamic NDE You'll Ever Read About 67

11. An Intriguing 1911 Near-Death Experience 75

12. A Science Professor Sees the Light. 81

13. The Man Who Fell Off Everest 85

14. An NDE on the Battlefield. 89

15. Retired Naval Architect Tells of His NDE 93

16. A Physician Discusses Her NDE Research 101

17. From Surgeon to Superman........................109

18. Has the NDE Been Debunked?.....................117

19. Researchers Offer More Light on the NDE..........123

20. Finding The Truth in The Light 129

21. Dr. Peter Fenwick Discusses Dying, Death
and Survival 135

22. Dr. Bruce Greyson Updates His NDE Research.......143

Epilogue: 10 Lessons Not Offered in
Sunday School or Science 101 149

References...155

About the Author 163

Preface

New and Old Light on the NDE

~

After Dr. Raymond Moody named the near-death experience (NDE) and created a worldwide interest in it with his 1975 classic, *Life After Life*, dozens of books followed. I have about 60 of them in my personal library. However, many of the authors, especially the researchers, did their best to avoid linking the phenomenon to the subject of life after death. When, some 20 years ago, I interviewed one leading researcher and questioned him on the survival aspect, he appeared somewhat offended by the question and replied that his objective was to study how the experience helped people better enjoy this life. I pondered on his comment, wondering if the NDE was nothing more than an escape mechanism. I further wondered about the value of research aimed at helping people escape from the realities of life, including what they believed to be the extinction of consciousness at death, as supported by the materialistic view. As I saw it, better enjoying this life was a result of recognizing this life as part of a larger life, thereby giving meaning to this life.

Another NDE researcher told me that his interest was in better understanding the dying process. Likewise, other academicians seemed to beat around the bush on the issue of consciousness surviving death. Apparently, it was too much of a religious subject, and science had impeached religion during the latter part of the nineteenth century. To suggest that their research supported religious beliefs was to invite disdain from their peers in science and academia. At least, that's how I interpreted it.

In the last few years, however, the leading researchers have come "off the fence," so to speak, and have clearly addressed the issue of life after death, although it is less religious and more scientific now to refer to it as "consciousness surviving death," or some such words, rather than to speak of heaven, life after death or the afterlife. It has taken nearly a half-century for the researchers to get off the fence. This is the "new" light referred to in the subtitle. The "old" light involves little known stories of "pre-Moody" NDEs that are in some respects more profound and dynamic than the newer ones.

This book is an anthology drawn from more than 400 blogs I have posted at the White Crow Books web site over the past 15 years. My blog is aimed at exploring the whole gamut of phenomena strongly suggesting that consciousness survives death in a larger life, but this collection, drawing from 23 of those blogs, is focused primarily on the near-death experience (NDE). Section I is fairly general in dealing with the existential and evidential aspects of survival, along with the skepticism accompanying the evidence, but the focus of Sections II, III, and IV is strictly on the NDE. Most of the articles in sections III and IV are based on personal interviews.

I do not write as a researcher, scientist, academician or near-death experiencer, simply as an old man with a fair amount of education and experience, as well as with a long-time interest in psychical research. My college education was mostly in journalism and my work experience primarily in insurance claims supervision and management, which involved examining and weighing evidence in civil litigation and potential litigation and then deciding whether to proceed to court or to attempt a compromise settlement. In 40 years of such employment, I came to understand courtroom science, including the absence of absolute certainty, and the many shades of gray that exist in nearly every observation, accident, or occurrence not subject to exact measurement. That understanding carried over to the evidence *for* and *against* the reality of psychic phenomena, including the NDE.

During those 40 years in the insurance claims field, extending to four countries and three states, and in the 23 years since retirement, I also worked as a freelance journalist, contributing more than 2,000 articles to at least 50 publication, while also authoring seven books, six on metaphysical subject and one on long-distance running, the latter a passion for many years. I served as editor of *The Journal for Spiritual and Consciousness Studies*, a quarterly publication of The Academy for Spiritual and Consciousness Studies, for five years, and also as editor of the Academy's magazine, *The Searchlight*, for 17 years.

Along the way, I devoted countless hours to studying psychical research and took a special interest in the research carried out by some esteemed scientists during the latter part of the nineteenth and early twentieth centuries. I came to the conclusion that their research offered overwhelming evidence that consciousness survives death, but I lamented the fact that so little of it was known to and understood by the general public. Unwittingly, I became something of an historian in the area of psychical research, contributing to several encyclopedias, including that of the Society for Psychical Research. The third article in Section I explains a little of that history. My efforts have been to interpret the old academic research and convert it to the language of the lay person.

Some minor editing, including changing titles and adding or deleting a paragraph here and there, has been done for this book, and therefore the articles that appear here do not always completely match those of the published blogs.

As noted, many of the articles/blogs in this book are based on personal interviews with both experiencers and researchers.

To my knowledge there have been no significant changes in the views expressed in those interviews or quoted from their books, but the reader needs to keep that possibility in mind. The dates the blogs were published online are shown at the beginning of each blog, or article. The only significant change I have observed, as stated above, is the trend by researchers to write about the survival of consciousness aspect of the NDE..

This book is intended primarily for seekers, especially those who are afflicted with what has been called "existential angst" – a condition resulting from finding no meaning in life and escaping from one's hopelessness with an over-indulgence in materialistic pursuits. As I see it, that is the underlying cause of all the chaos, turmoil, and insanity we appear to have in today's world. I believe that Giambattista Vico, an 18th-century Italian philosopher, hit the nail squarely on the head when he wrote that men first feel necessity, then look for utility, followed by comfort, then pleasure, and finally luxury, after which they finally go mad – when "each man is thinking of his own private interests." In that pursuit of pleasure and luxury, there is, according to Vico, a certain social disconnection, which involves moral, intellectual, and spiritual decline.

Michael Tymn
Kailua, Hawaii
January 2025

PART I

Examining the Existential, Evidential & Skeptical Aspects

"If man believes in nothing but the material world, he becomes a victim of the narrowness of his own consciousness. He is trapped in triviality."

—Emanuel Swedenborg

1

Taking Your Toys with You at Death

~

June 3, 2024

An aging friend who appears to be nearing the end of his life has become a very angry man recently. There was a time not long ago when he was very jovial as we talked over coffee or tea about such trivial matters as baseball and football, as if they are the most important things in the world. When I occasionally attempted to change the subject to spiritual concerns, he was quick to reject the topic and return to the real weighty sports stuff. I learned over time not to make any attempt at discussing spiritual matters and we recycled the sports topics over and over again. I don't know how many times he told me how great Mickey Mantle was or the distance of his longest homerun, but I know I don't have enough fingers on which to count them.

I offered my friend a copy of my book, *The Afterlife Revealed*, but he reacted with a sneer. The nature of his anger is difficult to identify, but I sense that he is mad at the world because he knows he is dying. As he has no real spiritual foundation, he apparently sees himself marching into an abyss of nothingness, i.e., total extinction, or perhaps into the humdrum or horrific afterworld offered by orthodox religions, and I suspect all that goes to the root cause of his anxiety and anger. Although most psychiatrists are apparently grounded in materialistic behaviorism and don't really seem to be familiar with it, my friend appears to be suffering from a disorder known as "existential angst." While his consciousness continues to strive to be one with his toys, his subconscious is nagging his conscious self to find some meaning in all of it, while driving across the point that he can't take his toys with him when he dies. It's that nagging that is bringing on the subtle and undiagnosed anxiety and anger.

No, I am not a psychiatrist or psychologist, but I've had enough experience with aging relatives, friends and acquaintances over my 88 years, along with extensive studies in psychical research, to have some clues as to what is happening. They are clues, nothing more. I may very well be wrong. I've come to the conclusion that absolute (100%) certainty on anything, including consciousness surviving death, is contraindicated for optimum mental health and that some doubt is necessary for us to deal with our challenges and progress in this lifetime.

All that is not to suggest that we should be lifetime skeptics and sit on the fence our entire lives, as so many insist on doing. I believe that seeking, searching, studying, striving, struggling, sacrificing, surrendering, and serving come before solving and soaring. Such a pursuit often leads from skepticism to conviction. Conviction does not mean absolute certainty, but it provides a confidence that borders on certainty and permits some peace of mind relative to life's meaning while avoiding much or all of the existential angst that seems to be affecting my friend.

I doubt that much of the of this subject is discussed in psychology classes. Such discussions would border on religion, a no-no subject in a scientific approach to mental health and well-being. Modern medicine wants none of that, nor does academia or the media. They don't grasp the difference between the dogma and doctrines of organized religions and the "indications" or "suggestions" we get from psychical research. Moreover, the media, clearly not understanding the difference, does not want to upset readers with "unscientific" subjects or even conflicting religious views. Better not to discuss the subject at all than risk censure by angry readers who are unable to reconcile such views with either their nihilistic or religious worldviews.

Being Philistines

As existentialist philosopher Søren Kierkegaard saw it: "If there were no eternal consciousness in a man, if at the foundation of all there lay only a wildly seething power which writhing with obscure passions produced everything that is great and everything that is insignificant, if a bottomless void never satiated lay hidden beneath all – what then would life be but despair?" Kierkegaard referred to those who took no interest in the subject as "philistines," and opined that they are in despair even if they don't realize it.

Or to quote the famous French philosopher, Michel De Montaigne: "They come and they go and they trot and they dance, and never a word about death. All well and good. Yet, when death does come – to them, their wives, their children, their friends – catching them unawares and unprepared, then what storms of passion overwhelm them, what cries, what fury, what despair!"

Actually, there *is* considerable anecdotal evidence suggesting that you can take your toys with you when you die. It's likely, however, that you won't know you are "dead" when you play with those toys. It's said to be as if you are stuck in a monotonous never-ending dream world. Those who scoff at such an idea might ask themselves if they know they are "alive" when they are dreaming at night. Such consciousness is clearly little understood by mainstream science, but many maverick scientists and scholars have studied the evidence for survival and to some extent what happens immediately after death. They include Alfred Russel Wallace, co-originator with Charles Darwin of the natural selection theory of evolution, Sir William Crookes, a world-renowned chemist of yesteryear, Sir Oliver Lodge, a physicist and pioneer in electricity and radio, on up to current near-death experience researchers such as Drs. Raymond Moody, Melvin Morse, and Bruce Greyson, to name only a few. Unfortunately, their views are suppressed by the mainstream. When they dare publish their unconventional or non-conformist findings, they become outlaws in their professions.

Believe it or not, there is even a little anecdotal evidence suggesting that there are "beings" in the afterlife environment who don't believe that humans or "earthlings" exist. Such weirdness boggles the mind and invites scoffs from those who assume that other dimensions of reality must resemble ours or believe that reductionistic science has it all figured out.

Many have abandoned beliefs about an afterlife because they assume that an old man with whiskers is calling the shots and allowing all kinds of bad things to happen to good people. They conclude that no loving "God" would permit such atrocities. They haven't stopped to consider that this life seems to be a small part of the larger life – one which is all about exercising free will in learning lessons by overcoming adversity. Nor do they consider that it is not necessary to have proof of God before accepting the evidence for survival. If there is a God overseeing it all, great, but if there are ballistic missiles headed our way, the president doesn't need to know their origin before ordering them shot down. Identifying the country of origin is secondary to accepting that they are headed our way. The same goes for the survival and God issues.

Even though psychical research, including NDE research, the subject of six of my seven published books, as well as about a dozen other books to which I have contributed, has nothing to do with religion, or even a belief in God, some of my non-religious friends think I am a "religious nut." I tell them that the books are essentially about consciousness and research strongly suggesting that consciousness survives death in a greater reality than the one we are now experiencing. However, the distinction between consciousness research and religious dogma is slow to sink in for most of them.

Agent of Satan

At the other extreme, some of my religious friends consider me an agent of Satan. Even though psychical research supports about 97 percent of their religious beliefs, especially the most critical one, life after death, it conflicts with some seemingly insignificant beliefs adopted by church authorities over the centuries, and these conflicts, they have been told, mean that it's all the work of the devil. Those researchers are all wolves in sheep's clothing, they claim.

I'll never make it on any best-seller list, but I'm satisfied with about 12,000 or so sales of the books. My best seller is *The Afterlife Revealed*, which is approaching 6,000 sales and now has 170 reviews at Amazon.com. I've had a number of people tell me that the book has made their terminal years much more endurable than it might have otherwise been had they been looking ahead to an abyss of nothingness. Some of my non-religious friends react with "one life at a time for me." I agree with them, but as the renowned psychiatrist Carl Gustav Jung put it, "A man should be able to say he has done his best to form a conception of life after death, or to create some image of it – even if he must confess his failure. Not to have done so is a vital loss." The problem is that most people don't recognize the loss until they are within shouting distance of what they think of as the abyss, at which point they scream in despair.

Even Sigmund Freud, who was not spiritually inclined, was concerned that one's attitude toward death has a bearing on his or her psychological health. "Is it not for us to confess that in our civilized attitude toward death, we are once more living psychologically beyond our means, and must reform and give truth its due?" he asked, while also reportedly telling a friend that if he had his life to live over again, he would pursue psychical research rather than psychiatry.

If I am interpreting those and other great thinkers correctly, the conscious self wants pleasure and luxury, but the subconscious (the soul) wants peace of mind, and that comes only with seeing this life as a part of a much larger one. Therein is the conflict that goes unrecognized by presidents, politicians, and the media. It is much easier for them to say that people are angry than to say they are in existential despair. If they suggest that people are in such despair, they have to explain what they are in despair over. It would not be politically, journalistically or scientifically correct to say that their materialistic lifestyles have detracted from their spiritual values and pursuits and that they have lost sight of the *larger life*. It is so much simpler to blame it on anger over economic deprivations and social injustices than to say it results from the pursuit of pleasure and luxury, the very things we think we want.

But back to the really important stuff. I agree that Mickey Mantle was a great player, but Willie Mays was a bit greater. Just my opinion.

2

NDE Researcher Sees Life as a Paradox

~

July 31, 2017

In her latest book, *A Manual for Developing Humans*, P. M. H. Atwater, a pioneer in near-death studies, points out that life is "inherently paradoxical." She defines paradox as "parallel principles that have crossed over." For example, "the only way you can keep love is to give it away." The one in her book that particularly jumped out at me is "the smarter we get, the dumber we are becoming."

Most people view death as a very negative experience, but as Atwater found out, there's a paradox here, too, since her three near "deaths" served her in a very positive way. They awakened her to a new reality. "Once back after my encounters with death, I continued to operate from 'realms of radiance' to the extent that everyday events and decisions lost significance," she explains early in the book. "The wisdom I returned with became more as stumbling blocks than guideposts (another paradox) until I regained my ability to discern differences – the contrast between 'here' and 'there' – between a practical application in the physical world and what I knew to be true in the greater worlds of spirit."

Atwater does not go into much detail about her three near-death experiences during the early months of 1977, the year she turned 40, as she told about those in her 1998 book, *Coming Back to Life*. This latest book touches upon all the things she was awakened to during her NDEs and in the 40 years of research that followed. It seemingly covers every conceivable subject relating to the human experience – intelligence, intuition, dreams, auras, synchronicity, health, nutrition, emotions, fears, pain, parenting, sex, soul mates, science, racism, terrorism, prophesies, planets, feminism, justice, politics, economics, messiahs, catastrophes, war, solar cycles, free will, death, enlightenment, quantum medicine, orgone energy. You name it and Atwater has some very interesting and intriguing ideas and suggestions about it.

As Atwater told me in an email exchange, her intent in writing the book was to cover all the basics for being/becoming fully human. "Being more spiritual is backwards thinking," she wrote. "Being all that you were born to be is the real goal in life, as it includes spirituality along with everything else. If we are fully ourselves, fully human, quite literally we are gods in the making." She added that just the day before sending the email, a man who had been told by his doctor that he would never walk again because of a serious leg condition, contacted her and told her that, as a result of reading her manual, rather "using" her manual, not just reading it, he has thrown away his crutches and canes and is now walking perfectly. She was also recently contacted by a therapist who told her that he is using her manual techniques throughout his practice.

"The manual is not channeled, doesn't come from any entity, angel, or spirit-type being," she explained. "It comes from my third near-death experience and what I called 'The Voice Like None Other.' No voice really. What seemed as if 'sound' later turned out to be the shimmer of The Void, entwined within the 80 years I spent testing existence itself."

Time of Extremes

Much of the manual has to do with change. "Sweeping changes are already flooding the earth plane and they will increase," she continued. "The United States, in its astrological birth chart, has a Pluto return set to occur in 2022. That ushers in a time of extremes – great strides forward along with what could be equally great disasters. I tell everyone to expect a four-year span of this patterning – from 2020 through 2024. My manual is made to order for this, because by showing people how to test themselves, prove to themselves how powerful and creative they are, they can then navigate changing times in a positive manner."

Atwater was quick to remind me that there is a paradox involved with all change, so that the "bad" may be for our betterment, while the "good" may really be to our detriment, at least in the short run. She cautions against "either/or judgment" and is convinced that there is no such thing as good and evil, as we are taught. She mentioned Ireland's new prime minister, Leo Varadkar. "He represents a break from the past. He's center-right who embraces and works with center-left. In a land that is staunchly Catholic, he is the son of a doctor who emigrated from Mumbai and a nurse from southeastern Ireland. He is gay, a man who has known since childhood he wanted to be a politician, and he meets everyone at their level – and not just in meeting rooms filled with cameras. Ireland today is flourishing because of his new kind of leadership, and in ways no one saw coming. The model he represents, a mixture of races, religions, sexual and political points of view, is beginning to emerge as a global phenomenon that crosses all borders and all mindsets."

Whether it is paradoxical or not, I am not sure, but Atwater cites a number of seemingly contradictory changes among today's children. She mentions that one-third of those children throughout the world who take the standard IQ test now score in the genius range of 150-160, most without genetic markers to account for this. However, there have been equal jumps in learning disorders. Moreover, one-third of young people today have little or no sense of living a full life and two-thirds have no intention of ever marrying, going to college, or becoming parents. One-third are amoral, with many of them too violent to handle. "These percentages wiggle around somewhat, depending on what source you check," she explained. "Yet, figures overall have remained fairly close to those I have given, for the last 15 years or so. This is impossible, clearly impossible, but it is happening consistently."

As Atwater sees it, many of today's young people are suffering emotionally due to difficulties in distinguishing between the real world and what they perceive from social media, the entertainment industry, and the advertising industry. "We need to at least acknowledge that there is something going on within the human family that is beyond our present understanding," she continued, suggesting that it is part of a rhythm, plan, perhaps even a divine plan, God. "If we can recognize the rhythms here, the patterns of change, then innovation can replace fear."

I asked Atwater if she had any thoughts about the tattoo craze among young people. She responded that she hadn't given that much thought, "except the obvious signs that humankind is seeking to be more tribal and sincerely desirous of being recognized as part of a chosen mindset, or pattern of mind." She further theorized that tattoos are a visual affirmation of one having chosen his or her family, how each individual wants to feel, to respond to life, to be recognized above and beyond whatever seems "fated" from the bloodlines of birth.

I asked her what she would do if she could go back in time to her younger years with what she has learned over the past 40 years. "I'd go back to my childhood and forgive my mother and myself," she responded. "Until we can face our youngest years, all the pain, all the joy, all the mystery, all the confusion, we're handicapping ourselves [if we hold on to it]. Progress means nothing if it's hollow, and hollow it is until we can forgive what seemed limiting. Life reflects thought. Our ability to love and to forgive marks the difference between thoughts around and within us and what actually has value."

The Great Shifting

Back to those "sweeping changes" that Atwater sees from 2020 through 2024, I sensed something of a doomsday scenario from what she set forth in her manual and asked her what she would tell young people now about raising a family, pursuing goals, etc. "I cannot imagine any reason not to love, dream, plan, try, look ahead," she replied. "Knowing about where we are in the grand cycle of time, I believe makes a difference in our sanity, in understanding our place in the world and what's going on around us. Like it or not, our world, our planet, is experiencing what is called 'The Great Shifting' or 'The Turning of the Cosmic Clock.' This massive changeover in energy flow happens every 25,920 years. On top of that, two great ages of time are now on top of each other: The Age of Pisces and The Age of Aquarius. This 'overlap' is crazy in how ideas clash and in how we are called upon to make decisions and take action in ways which are unprecedented. No matter how wild or unstable things seem, there really is progress; we are moving forward and upward in the Grand Cycles of Time."

Atwater's son once asked her how he is supposed to recognize truth. Her reply: "When everyone agrees with each other, and there is no dissent, run for the nearest door and get out. All you have found is illusion. But when you find paradox of unity in opposition, stay as long as you can and learn as much as you can. You have found truth."

3

Overwhelming Evidence for
the Survival of Consciousness

~

July 28, 2023

In my award-winning essay for the Bigelow Essay competition of 2021, I attempted to make a legal case for life after death having been proved with overwhelming evidence by 1900. I argued that the legal doctrine of *Res Judicata*, meaning "it has already been decided," should be applied to the cumulative evidence gathered between 1850 and 1900, and therefore should not require another legal action. Case closed! The issue for this blog is whether 1900 was a realistic year. Was the case for survival made before that or perhaps later, or not at all.

In my simulated court trial, I offered the testimony of 11 witnesses, including Judge John Edmonds, Dr. George Dexter, Governor Nathaniel Tallmadge, Professor Robert Hare, Professor James Mapes, Professor Alfred Russel Wallace, Sir William Crookes, Sir William Barrett, Rev. William Stainton Moses, Dr. Richard Hodgson, and Sir Oliver Lodge, quoting from their reports and books on their psychical research as if they were testifying at a trial. I wanted to include Professor James Hyslop, perhaps the most knowledgeable of them all, but the 25,000 word limit for the essay prevented that. Hyslop's research took place mostly between 1905 and 1920, nearly all after the research by those 11 witnesses, and so he was the one omitted and the line was drawn at 1900 rather than 1920.

Needless to say, the more evidence the better, and had I gone to 1920 and beyond to the present, it would have made for an even stronger case, but I was forced by the "court" to make my case within those 25,000 words. In my closing argument, I mentioned that I could have called many more witnesses to the stand, but if the testimonies of those 11 esteemed men weren't convincing to the jury members, then it was likely that 22 witnesses wouldn't convince them. Had I been able to continue beyond 1920, I would definitely have included the research conducted between 1975 and the present relative to the near-death experience. It also offers overwhelming evidence that we are more than our physical bodies. The NDE evidence would have been icing on the cake.

My simulated court trial involved a civil action, not a criminal one, and therefore the standard involved was a "preponderance of evidence," meaning that the evidence *for* outweighed the evidence *against*, a significantly easier standard than that of "beyond a reasonable doubt," required by criminal courts and by the contest rules. It didn't seem appropriate to apply the criminal standard to the case for survival, as it came across as a defensive measure, so I substituted "overwhelming evidence" to mean the same thing as the desired standard of "beyond a reasonable doubt." In exchange for the extra burden of the higher standard and the fact that the attorney for the survivalists was not introducing evidence beyond 1900, except for one reported by Barrett involving a levitation, the attorney arguing for the nihilists agreed to give the survivalists a bit more latitude in their testimony.

Catch 22 Situation

The year 1930 seems like a more reasonable cut-off, as that's when parapsychology began to replace psychical research. The change appears to have been prompted by the disagreements of a number of researchers over investigations of three mediums – Mina Crandon, aka "Margery," George Valiantine, and Rudi Schneider – during the mid and late 1920s. It became increasingly clear from those investigations that "spirit" activity through mediums was not an acceptable explanation for hard-core scientists. It was a Catch 22 situation. If no other explanation than spirits, it had to be fraud. Even those who supported the spirit explanation for the phenomena had to beat around the bush in stating their conclusions, avoiding as much as possible any reference to spirits. Thus, parapsychology limited its scope to extra-sensory perception (ESP) and psychokinesis (PK) while avoiding any discussion of spirits and survival.

But drawing the line at 1930 would exclude some very impressive and meaningful research with mediums carried out by Dr. T. Glen Hamilton, of Canada, until his death in April 1935. So an argument can be made that 1935 is a more appropriate year at which to say that the case for survival was fully made.

Here are conclusions, their exact words, offered in the "trial" by seven of the witnesses named above. It should be kept in mind that these witnesses were not casual observers of the phenomena they reported on; they carried out countless experiments with various mediums over a number of years. Hodgson, for example, studied Leonora Piper for some 18 years and on the average of three times a week. Moreover, all the researchers were fully aware of the various debunking theories.

Testimonials

By Hare, professor of chemistry at the University of Pennsylvania and world-renowned inventor:

I sincerely believe that I have communicated with the spirits of my parents, sister, brother, and dearest friends, and likewise with the spirits of the illustrious Washington and other worthies of the spirit world; that I am by them commissioned, under their auspices, to teach truth and to expose error.

By Mapes, a professor of chemistry at The American Institute and renowned inventor:

The manifestations which are pertinent to the ends required are so conclusive in their character as to establish in my mind certain cardinal points. These are: First, there is a future state of existence, which is but a continuation of our present state of being...Second, that the great aim of nature, as shown through a great variety of spiritual existences is progression, extending beyond the limits of this mundane sphere...Third, that spirits can and do communicate with mortals, and in all cases evince a desire to elevate and advance those they commune with.

By Wallace, biologist and co-originator with Charles Darwin of the natural selection theory of evolution:

The spiritual theory is the logical outcome of the whole of the facts. Those who deny it, in every instance with which I am acquainted, either from ignorance or disbelief, leave half the facts out of view.

By Barrett, professor of physics at the Royal College of Science and renowned inventor:

I am personally convinced that the evidence we have published decidedly demonstrates (1) the existence of a spiritual world, (2) survival after death, and (3) of occasional communication from those who have passed over.

By Crookes, a physicist and chemist who discovered the element thallium and was a pioneer in radioactivity:

> [The phenomena] point to the existence of another order of human life continuous with this, and demonstrate the possibility in certain circumstances of communication between this world and the next.

By Lodge, professor of physics, a pioneer in electricity and radio, and president of the British Association for the Advancement of Science:

> I tell you with all my strength of the conviction which I can muster that we do persist, that people still continue to take an interest in what is going on, that they know far more about things on this earth than we do, and are able from time to time to communicate with us…I do not say it is easy, but it is possible, and I have conversed with my friends just as I can converse with anyone in this audience now.

By Hodgson, lecturer in philosophy at Cambridge and later the first full-time psychical researcher:

> I had but one object, to discover fraud and trickery. Frankly, I went to Mrs. Piper with Professor James of Harvard University about twelve years ago with the object of unmasking her…I entered the house profoundly materialistic, not believing in the continuance of life after death; today I say I believe. The truth has been given to me in such a way as to remove from me the possibility of a doubt.

Although Hyslop, who taught philosophy, ethics and logic at Columbia University before becoming a full-time psychologist and psychical researcher, did not testify because of the court limits on time, his deposition was taken before the trial and he stated:

> Personally, I regard the fact of survival after death as scientifically proved. I agree that this opinion is not upheld in scientific quarters. But this is neither our fault nor the fault of the facts. Evolution was not believed until long after it was proved. The fault lay with those who were too ignorant or too stubborn to accept the facts. History shows that every intelligent man who has gone into this investigation, if he gave it adequate examination at all, has come out believing in spirits; this circumstance places the burden of proof on the shoulders of the skeptic.

If we consider the research by Hare, Mapes, Edmonds, Dexter, and Tallmadge, not to mention French educator Allan Kardec and American clergyman Adin Ballou, we can conclude that the case for consciousness surviving death was made before 1860. Add in Wallace and we can draw the line at 1865.

No Secondary Personality

Then again, we might put the year at 1892. That was the year that a "spirit" claiming to have been George Pellew began communicating through the mediumship of Leonora Piper. Until then, many researchers, including Hodgson and Professor William James of Harvard, who recruited Hodgson to head up the American branch of the Society for Psychical Research in 1887, accepted the genuineness of much of the phenomena but leaned toward a belief that the so-called "spirits" were secondary personalities buried in the medium's subconscious, and that these secondary personalities could somehow access information telepathically, even at a great distance, or from some kind of "cosmic reservoir" not yet known to science (which later came to be called *Super Psi* or *Living Agent Psi*). As far-fetched as it seemed, it was more "scientific" than communication from spirits of the dead. The idea of spirits was seen as a return to the follies and superstitions of religion, which had been impeached by science during the 1860s.

However, Pellew, who died in an accident in New York City at age 32, during February 1892, and began communicating through the entranced Piper some six weeks later, demonstrated all the characteristics of the man he claimed to have been in the material world and otherwise displayed too much personality to have been some second-self pretender buried away in Piper's subconscious. "To the person unfamiliar with a series of [sittings with Mrs. Piper], it may seem a plausible hypothesis that perhaps one secondary personality might do the whole work, might use the voice and write contemporaneously with the hand," Hodgson wrote. "I do not, however, think it at all likely that he would continue to think it plausible after witnessing and studying the numerous coherent groups of memories connected with different persons, the characteristic emotions, tendencies distinguishing such different persons, the excessive complication of acting required, and the absence of any apparent bond of union for the associated thoughts and feelings indicative of each individuality, save some persistent basis of that individuality itself." Other researchers agreed with Hodgson, although James, perhaps out of concern for sanctioning something too much like religion, which science had already impeached, sat on the fence."

Too Much Humbug

The basic problem was that there was too much "bosh," too much "humbug" too much "twaddle," too many conflicting ideas, coming through many mediums, probably the majority of mediums, even some of the better mediums, such as Mrs. Piper. Over time, the dedicated researchers were able to filter all this conflicting material out of the communication and still find veridical information outside the scope of fraud, coincidence, chance guessing, whatever theory opposed spirit communication. While religions had led people to believe that those in the spirit world, one they called "heaven," are all-powerful and all-knowing, the research suggested that this is definitely not the case. The researchers discovered that most "spirits" on the other side know little, if anything, more than they did in the physical world. Moreover, the lower and less-advanced spirits, being at a lower vibration and closer to the earth vibration, were better able to communicate than the advanced spirits. Among those lower spirits were some with malevolent intentions.

Whether the spirits communicating were advanced and benevolent or lowly and malevolent, the early research definitely provided overwhelming evidence that consciousness survives death. I'll stick with the case for survival having been made by 1900. *Res Judicata.*

4

Experiencing a Pre-Death Life Review

~

July 15, 2024

A number of people have reported a "life review" during a near-death experience (NDE) – seeing every second of their lives flash before them in what might be called a timeless moment. A man named Tom Sawyer had an NDE in 1978, one in which he recalled living every thought and attitude connected with decisive moments in his life and seeing them through the eyes of those affected by his actions. Popular NDE author PMH Atwater reported that she saw every thought she had ever had, every word she had ever spoken, and every deed she had ever done.

A long-time friend, the late Donald Morse, a Temple University science professor, recalled seeing his whole life flash before him, including temper tantrums as a child, his victory in a dart-throwing contest, a hospital bout with colitis, asthma attacks, family visits, throwing a player out at home plate, shooting a winning basket, crying when the New York Giants lost a game, seeing his father die from lung cancer, getting married, seeing his three children born, doing a surgical procedure on the day

President Kennedy was killed, receiving a Temple University research award, as well as many other events in his life. (His NDE is further described under Section III.)

Physicist and author Dr. James Beichler speculates that a person who has a highly developed spiritual consciousness – one that has kept pace with the development of his mind – may not need a life review as the person has reviewed his or her life while in the flesh. Although I don't know how developed my spiritual consciousness is, I attempted such a life review one night recently when I had a difficult time sleeping, hoping that it is a time-saver after I transition to the larger world. My focus was on the negative experiences rather than the positive. Those I left for another sleepless night.

Fortunately, I couldn't recall any murders, thefts, or whatever else that might be classified as a felonious act. The word "bully" wasn't really in my vocabulary when I was a kid during the 1940s, but one of the first things I recalled was acting like a bully with another kid my age. It was over a ridiculously trivial matter. If my after-death life review is like Tom Sawyer's, I will feel myself being punched in the nose by my own fist. But hopefully the remorse I now feel for my one "bully" act is enough to avoid seeing it in a life review.

I recall rationing during World War II, in particular Super Suds, a laundry soap. My mother said that the amount allowed by the government was not enough for our laundry, and so I somehow cheated the system and managed to get two boxes of Super Suds at the store. I don't recall how I did it, but I can still picture my mother's joyous expression when I brought two boxes home. I need to feel more remorse for that one. What if some other person didn't get his or her one box because I got two?

Being a practicing Catholic during my youth, I abstained from eating meat every Friday. However, there was one Friday when I attended a baseball game and couldn't resist having a hot dog. As I munched into it, I wondered how many days I'd have to spend in the fires of purgatory because of my lack of discipline. Now that meat is permitted on Friday, I'm hopeful that all prior sins in this regard are pardoned.

In the fifth grade at Catholic school, each class contributed to a stage program. Ours was a tribute to singer Al Jolson and involved singing "Way down upon the Swannee River." We all had to darken our faces with burnt cork, just like Jolson. There was nothing racist about it that I could see then or now, but today it would be considered by some to be a terribly racist thing. As I see it, applying current standards to past activities of spiritual evolution is part of the insanity we are now experiencing, and I'm confident that it will not come up in my life review.

"Culturism" was more common than racism where I grew up and various relatives and friends had derogatory names for people from three or four European countries. I do remember choosing not to use any of those names and fully respecting natives of those countries. Perhaps I can get points for that in my review.

Fewer Temptations

Without television, we had fewer temptations in those days. We weren't exposed to carnal scenes or foul language at home, or even in the movies that we attended once a week. I wonder if those responsible for popularizing such influences today will see the effects of it all in their life reviews. Then again, perhaps it has just provided challenges and learning experiences.

Jumping ahead to my adult years, I recall climbing a coconut tree on private property and pulling off a coconut for personal consumption. I don't think I considered it as thievery at the time, but, in retrospect, it might be called that. I still have that theft memorialized in a photograph and hope the statute of limitations has run on it.

I further remember visiting my parents and using their car to go to the grocery store. Not being able to find an open parking stall in the parking lot, I decided to take advantage of my father's handicap placard and pulled into a stall reserved for the truly handicapped. I justified my act by reasoning that I had Achilles tendonitis at the time, a result of too much competitive running. Also, there was another handicap stall available. That violation remained with me for a day or two, but I don't know if that was enough remorse. It may be that during a real-life review I will see a handicapped person unable to find a parking stall, then driving out of the parking lot and having a serious accident, all because I had used the parking stall he would have had were it not for my selfishness.

I remembered the time that I copied something protected by copyright law and passed it on to several friends. Shame on me. Also, I recall renting a movie at a Blockbuster store and then lending it to a friend to see the movie, thereby cheating the store out of a possible rental to my friend. When I heard that our Blockbuster franchise was closing, I wondered if I had contributed to it.

Extermination

Perhaps the most difficult dilemma for me and many others is where to draw the line on exterminating low-life creatures, i.e., house pests. I've swatted hundreds of flies over my lifetime and ended the lives of thousands of ants and termites. Add in some cockroaches, mice, rats and geckos, the latter especially rampant on the walls here in Hawaii. If, as Tom Sawyer experienced it, I have to feel the effects of eliminating those creatures, I'm really in trouble. I'll be eaten alive during my review. I consider it every time I hear my wife scream and then arm myself with a flyswatter, all the while weighing the unsanitary effects of allowing the creatures to run about or fly free about the house against eliminating them. A friend told me that his wife, apparently a mystic of some kind, talks to the creatures and becomes friends with them, but I am not gifted in that respect, nor is my wife.

I often look back on my competitive running days with much fondness, but Gina, my wife, does not share in my memories. She reminds me that after we both came home from our jobs in those earlier years, she was laboring away with household chores, especially cooking, while I was out running around the streets for my daily workout. I should have been home helping with the cooking, cleaning, child care, whatever. Because I couldn't run on a full stomach, it was necessary for me to do the workout before the evening meal, not after, so it more or less boiled down to giving up the activity completely or continuing in my selfish ways. There was really little room for compromise, but since Gina apparently recognized how important that activity was to my mental and physical health, she never pushed it and I remained ignorant of my selfishness until later years. I was a victim of my ancestors' mindset that women did all the cooking. I don't think my father even cooked toast. If, in my self-judgment, I am faced with justifying my pursuit of sport for an hour a day, I hope my higher self agrees with the way I did it. Otherwise, I could find myself on a treadmill to hell.

There are things I have not mentioned or have forgotten, so I may face a life review in spite of attempting to do it before death. But what's the point of saving time if there is no time in that realm?

5

Dealing with Doubting
Thomas Syndrome

~

March 18, 2019

E ven though I have long followed the sport of track & field,
I shake my head in disbelief when I look at the eight-foot
ceiling in my house and try to visualize someone jumping
over a bar that high. Yet, I know that the world record in the
high jump is eight-feet, one-half inch, by Javier Sotomayor of
Cuba, set on July 27, 1993. I didn't see that world-record jump,
but I can believe it, as I've seen other humans jump three or
four inches under that height and I am familiar with the high
standards of officiating in the sport. I don't have to see it to
believe it.

However, I have encountered countless skeptics who refuse
to believe in certain psychic phenomena because they can't do
it themselves, because they've never witnessed it, or because
it defies the laws of materialistic science. They suffer from
"Doubting Thomas Syndrome," so-called because the apostle
Thomas refused to believe in the resurrected Christ until he

could touch his wounds. I'll admit that many things in the psychic realm which I've read or heard about exceed my boggle threshold and so I am skeptical to some degree or another. But when I read the testimony of distinguished scientists and scholars who have witnessed it countless times under controlled conditions, my skepticism begins to erode toward belief. Then again, when I see illusionists pull off amazing tricks on television, such as on "The Carbonaro Effect," I begin to wonder if somehow those researchers were victims of some very clever illusionists.

I'll usually reason my way back to a high degree of belief in the phenomenon by concluding that there is manipulation of some kind going on with the photography that the home viewer can't see, but I continue to wonder how the victims of the trick on television are so easily duped. While I can accept that even world-renowned scientists, such as Sir William Crookes, who claimed to have witnessed floating accordions, levitations, and other amazing phenomena with medium D. D. Home, could have been duped a time or two, I struggle to believe that he and so many intelligent men and women could have been fooled dozens, even hundreds of times.

Professor Charles Richet, a Nobel Prize winner in medicine, claimed to have witnessed medium Eusapia Palladino more than 200 times. "Even if there were no other medium than Eusapia in the world, her manifestations would suffice to establish scientifically the reality of telekinesis and ectoplasmic forms," said Richet, who also observed phenomena with many other mediums. "Yes, it is absurd; but no matter – it is true," Richet asserted. It should be noted that even though Richet was certain no trickery was involved, he still refused to believe in spirits. He preferred to think of it as some kind of subconscious workings of the medium's mind.

My friend Doug is also a long-time follower of track & field and has even written books about "unbelievable" feats in the athletic arena. He has no difficulty in accepting an eight-foot high jump, but he refuses to believe that anybody can bend a spoon without applying physical force. He believes that all reports of such a phenomenon are just so much hooey. Doug is a big fan of James "The Amazing" Randi and recalls that Randi supposedly exposed British psychic Uri Geller's sleight of hand in spoon-bending on television some years ago. As I recall, there is another side to that story, but I don't remember exactly what it is and I am not interested enough to research it.

Mind over Matter

About 15 years ago, I attended a conference in which a medium (I think it was Anne Gehman) gave a spoon-bending demonstration and then had forks and spoons distributed to all in the audience, around a hundred people. I don't recall the ritual that the medium led us all through, but I believe it was something like closing our eyes and gently rubbing the neck of the spoon or fork between the thumb and the forefinger while visualizing it bending. However, I do recall that more than half the people in the audience, including my wife, Gina, had spoons and forks curl up on them without physical force being applied. Several people, including the woman sitting to my right, had the four prongs on the forks they were holding curl up into tight knots. I confess to being one of the failures that night.

When I told Doug about what I had observed at that conference, he still refused to believe it possible. The closed eyes and the light finger rubbing suggested fraud to him. He asked that Gina demonstrate the next time we visit his neck of the woods. I told him that she really hasn't tried to bend a spoon since then, but I'm pretty sure that if she were to try it again in front of him that she would fail. Doug saw my reply as an admission that we were somehow duped, even though we don't know how we were duped. When I told him we still had the spoon, he suggested we have a metallurgical test done on it and we would discover that it was a special cheap metal that bent from the friction generated by the heat from the light rubbing.

If you put "spoon-bending" into an Internet search, you'll get the skeptic's view on how it is done while also finding a few explanations suggesting real telekinetic or psychokinetic powers, or mind over matter. One such site states that you have to "be one with spoon" and feel the energy between your fingers.

I don't know how the spoons curl up, but I am more inclined to accept some mind-over-matter explanation, possibly greatly enhanced by the group energy, over cheap metal. The four prongs curling up on the fork held by the person sitting to my right is ten times more mind-boggling to me than the curling of the spoon, especially since the woman's fingers were supposed to be rubbing the neck of the fork and not the prongs. It would have required some long-nose plyers and much more time to curl up those prongs in tight knots if I were to attempt it. The skeptic will likely conclude that the woman was a "plant" by the medium. If so, there were many such plants in the audience.

Concerns

I can't explain it, but I do know that Gina was not trying to trick anybody and I am reasonably certain that the woman sitting next to me was not part of an act. I'm not a Doubting Thomas. If I were a Doubting Thomas, here are the questions I would have regarding that eight-foot high jump:

- How come Sotomayor never replicated that world-record jump?
- How come *nobody* has replicated it in more than a quarter century?
- How do we know the officials weren't bribed by the Castro regime of Cuba?
- Did each of the officials have proper training in measuring techniques? Did at least one of them have a Ph.D. in mathematics?

- How do we know that the officials weren't drugged and weren't hallucinating?
- Could the officials have been hypnotized to think they were seeing 96.5 inches on the measuring device?
- How do we know that the measuring device wasn't 'doctored' beforehand and off a few inches?
- Is the measuring device still available for calibration? If it is, how can we be sure it is the same one used 26 years ago?
- Was Sotomayor tested for performance-enhancing drugs? If so, could he have used one of those drugs that defies testing? Might the drug testers have been bribed?
- Did anyone check Sotomayor's shoes for hidden springs?
- Could an illusionist have been employed to make it appear that he cleared the bar when he actually went under it?

Is there anything we can accept as absolute truth? As I see it, there are four classes of skeptics:

The Seeker: This is the true skeptic, open-minded and searching for truth, recognizing the interconnectedness between science and spirituality. Often, the seeker becomes a "believer" but retains some degree of skepticism as he or she understands the difference between evidence and proof while recognizing that *absolute* proof is rare in any scientific endeavor. He or she also recognizes conflicting non-mechanistic explanations for various phenomena. Many of the pioneers of psychical research were in this category. Unfortunately, many seekers are restrained somewhat by ego and/or the fear of being ridiculed in going public with their beliefs.

The Shrugger: This person is so caught up in worldly matters as to be indifferent to other-worldly truths. She would much rather escape into a novel than explore metaphysical truths. He'd rather talk about babes, booze, and ballgames than discuss psychic phenomena. For the most part, the shrugger is a philistine – a person indifferent to the existential – and hasn't really examined the evidence for or against paranormal phenomena but simply wants to appear "intelligent" by wearing the skeptic's badge.

The Smirker: This person thinks of him- or herself as too mentally gifted or advanced to believe in anything that is not subject to strict scientific "proof," all the while failing to recognize that science has always lagged behind truth and that very few things supposedly "proved" by science are in fact proved with *absolute* certainty. Quite often, this person is a product of a strict religious upbringing but his fertile mind was later enlightened by pompous college professors, thereby supporting his rebellious attitude toward his religious parents. The smirker is to science what the fundamentalist is to religion. He is stuck on the strictness of the scientific method as much as the religious fundamentalist is stuck on a literal interpretation of the Bible. The smirker is "born again" in science and a fundamentalist in scientism. Paranormal phenomena are simply beyond the smirker's boggle threshold and there is no way his ego will permit him to be wrong again, as he was when he believed in Santa Claus and the Easter Bunny.

The Scoffer: The scoffer, or cynic, is simply a smirker in the extreme, often a militant atheist. Waving the banner of science, these militants fancy themselves self-appointed guardians of truth in the war on superstition. Rather than just react to his friend's belief in paranormal phenomena with an arrogant smirk or snicker, the scoffer relentlessly goes on the attack, often sneering and demanding that others conform to his or her strict science code. Some scoffers demand a total separation of the spiritual and the secular, insisting that prayer be removed from the classroom, that the Bible be removed from the courtroom, that references to God be removed from the currency and public institutions. He or she confuses or doesn't understand the difference between religious dogma/doctrine and spirituality. The scoffer is a closed-minded pseudoskeptic, i.e., pretend skeptic.

PART II

Historical NDEs

"To those who know the truth of facts, and who do not know what can and cannot be – at least out of the exact sciences – it will appear on reflection that the most probable direction of inquiry, the best chance of eliciting a satisfactory result, is that which is suggested by the spirit hypotheses. I mean the hypothesis that some intelligence, which is not that of any human being clothed in flesh and blood, has a direct share in the phenomena."

—**Augustus De Morgan**

6

Admiral Tells of Drowning and What Happened After

~

December 13, 2010

Pseudoskeptics and debunkers claim that lack of oxygen to the brain explains the tunnel effect reported by many people who have had a near-death experience (NDE) and that the other things reported are a product of fantasy, imagination, hallucination, and expectations. Before Dr. Raymond Moody named the NDE and popularized it in his 1975 best-selling book *Life After Life,* very few people were aware of the phenomenon and so there was little, if any, expectation. Now that many books on the subject have been published the expectation factor is more of a consideration. That is, the pseudoskeptics can now claim that people have been "programmed" to imagine similar experiences. And so it is that some of the very old NDEs give credibility to the newer ones, since those experiencers were likely not expecting anything.

I recently came across a very interesting NDE involving a very credible person, one not likely to have made up such a story. It was in an 1863 book, *From Matter to Spirit*, authored by Sophia Elizabeth De Morgan, the wife of the renowned British mathematician and logician Augustus De Morgan, who wrote a lengthy preface to the book setting forth his 10 years of experience in investigating psychic phenomena.

The NDE was reported by British Rear Admiral Sir Francis Beaufort (1774-1857), who is most remembered today for devising the Beaufort Wind Scales. After his retirement from the Royal Navy, Beaufort served as a council member of the Royal Society, the Royal Observatory, and the Royal Geographic Society, the latter of which he was a founding member. After telling his experience to his physician, a Dr. Wollaston, he was asked to provide a detailed account in writing.

The experience took place sometime around 1795, when he was a young sailor on one of His Majesty's ships in Portsmouth harbor. Beaufort wrote that he was sculling about in a small boat endeavoring to fasten the boat to a ship when he stepped upon the gunwale, lost his balance, and fell into the water. Not knowing how to swim, he splashed about before he began to sink below the surface. "All hope had fled, all exertion ceased, and I felt that I was drowning," Beaufort related in the lengthy letter to Dr. Wollaston. While his plight came to the attention of others, it took a minute or two for them to reach him.

Beaufort went on to say that one would assume that a drowning person is too much occupied in the struggle or too much absorbed by alternate hope and despair to remember what happened. "Not so, however, with the fact which immediately ensued," he wrote. "My mind had then undergone the sudden revolution which appeared to you (Wollaston) so remarkable, and all the circumstances of which are now so vividly fresh in my memory as if they had occurred but yesterday."

He continued the story: "From the moment that all exertion had ceased – which I imagine was the immediate consequence of complete suffocation – a calm feeling of the most perfect tranquility succeeded the most tumultuous sensation. It might be called apathy, certainly not resignation; for drowning no longer appeared an evil; I no longer thought of being rescued, nor was I in any bodily pain. On the contrary, my sensations were now of rather a pleasurable cast, partaking of that dull but contented sort of feeling which precedes the sleep produced by fatigue. Though the senses were thus deadened, not so the mind; its activity seemed to be invigorated in a ratio which defies all description; for thought rose after thought with a rapidity of succession that is not only indescribably, but probably inconceivable, by anyone who has been himself in a similar situation. The course of these thoughts I can even now in a great measure retrace: the event that had just taken place, the awkwardness which produced it – the bustle it must have occasioned, for I had observed two persons jump from the chains – the effect it would have on a most affectionate father, the manner in which he would disclose it to the rest of the family, and thousand other circumstances minutely associated with home, were the first series of reflections that occurred."

His life then played back before him. "Our last cruise – a former voyage and shipwreck – my school, the progress I had made there, the time had misspent, and even all my boyish pursuits and adventures. Thus, traveling backwards, every incident of my past life seemed to me to glance across my recollection in retrograde procession; not, however, in mere outline as here stated, but the picture filled up with every minute and collateral feature; in short, the whole period of my existence seemed to be placed before me in a kind of panoramic view, and each act of it seemed to be accompanied by a consciousness of right or wrong, or by some reflection on its cause of consequence – indeed many trifling events, which had been long forgotten, then crowded into my imagination, and with the character of recent familiarity."

Infinite Power

Beaufort then speculated on the meaning of it all. "May not all this be some indication of the almost infinite power of memory with which we may awaken in another world, and be compelled to contemplate our past lives? Or might it not, in some degree, warrant the inference that death is only a change or modification of our existence, in which there is no real pause or interruption? But however that may be, one circumstance was highly remarkable, that the innumerable ideas which floated into my mind were all retrospective; yet I had been religiously brought up; my hopes and fears of the next world had lost nothing of their early strength, and at any other period intense interest and awful anxiety would have been excited by the mere idea that I was floating on the threshold of eternity; yet at that inexplicable moment, when I had full consciousness that I had already crossed that threshold, not a single thought wandered into the future; I was wrapped entirely in the past. The length of time that was occupied by this deluge of ideas, or rather the shortness of time into which they were condensed, I cannot now state with precision; yet, certainly, two minutes could not have elapsed from the moment of suffocation to the time of my being hauled up."

Author De Morgan noted that such reports after sudden death are rare, but that there are many similar stories related by those dying from prolonged illness. "...the soul often returns to the scenes of childhood, and seems to wander with its first friends in the earliest home. But a few hours before death not only is the presence of already gone friends discerned, but perceptions of beautiful scenery, sounds of exquisite music, and sometimes even the objects required for a long journey, seem to be present to the mind of the departing traveler...It is as if the walls of the prison giving way, the captive before his escape looks sometimes through one, and sometimes another opening, into the region beyond, whence the friendly inhabitants some to guide him on his way."

The experience of Horace Abraham Ackley, M.D., of Cleveland, Ohio reported by De Morgan was not a near-death experience. It was an actual experience as communicated through a medium. Ackley reported: "I experienced but very little suffering during the last few days of my life, though at first there were struggles, and my features were distorted; but I learned, after my spirit had burst its barriers and was freed from its connection with the external body, that these were produced by it in an attempt to sever this connection, which in all cases is more or less difficult; the vital points of contact being suddenly broken by disease, the union in other portions of the system is necessarily severed with violence, but, as far as I have learned, without consciousness of pain. Like many others, I found that I was unable to leave the form at once. I could feel myself gradually raised from my body, and in a dreamy, half-conscious state. It seemed as though I was not a united being – that I was separated into parts, and yet despite of this there seemed to be an indissoluble connecting link. My spirit was freed a short time after the organs of my physical body had entirely ceased to perform their functions. My spiritual form was then united into one, and I was raised a short distance above the body, standing over it by what power I was unable to tell. I could see those who were in the room around me, and knew by what was going on that a considerable time must have elapsed since dissolution had taken place, and I presume I must have been for a time unconscious; and this I find is a common experience, not however, universal."

Life Review

Ackley then reported his life review. "As consciousness returned to me, the scenes of my whole life seemed to move before me like a panorama; every act seemed as though it were drawn in life size and was really present; it was all there, down to the closing scenes. So rapidly did it pass, that

I had little time for reflection. I seemed to be in a whirlpool of excitement; and then, just as suddenly as this panorama had been presented, it was withdrawn, and I was left without a thought of the past or future to contemplate my present condition. I looked around me, and I thought, if there is a possibility of spirits (for I seemed half-conscious now that I was a spirit) manifesting themselves to those still in the form, how gladly would I now do so, and thereby inform my friends and others of my condition, at least as far as I understood it myself, which I confess was not very far. Everything seemed to be in a whirl of motion; scarcely had one desire come, before another was presented. I said to myself, 'Death is not so bad a thing after all, and I should like to see what the country is that I am going to, if I am a spirit."

Ackley recalled hearing that guardian spirits are there to welcome the newly arrived soul, but he saw none. "Scarcely had this thought passed through my mind, when two, with whom I was unacquainted, but toward whom I was attracted, appeared before me. They were men of intelligence, but like myself, had given no special attention to the higher principles of spirituality; they knew my name, although I did not reveal it, and they shook hands with me in a hail-fellow-well-met sort of way, that was very pleasant to me.

The two spirits then conducted Ackley from the room in which he had died. "Everything around me seemed shadowy, yet through these shadows they conducted me to a place where there were a number of spirits assembled.; these had been in spirit life a longer time than I had....I remained in conversation with these spirits for some time, and then, without knowing why or how, I was attracted back to the place in which my spirit had separated itself from the form. I then found that I must have been in their company much longer than I supposed, as, contrary to the experience of many whom I have since met, I did not attend my own funeral; and I would here remark, that it is generally gratifying to a spirit to do this, and where the body can be kept for some time, they gladly embrace the opportunity of attending on this ceremony, and listening to and aiding those who officiate on such occasions."

De Morgan cites another case in which a communicating spirit explained that the difficulty a spirit has in freeing itself from the physical body is in proportion to its "lower desires."

7

The Most Profound NDE ever?

～

November 18, 2013

Although the near-death experience (NDE) was not so named until the 1970s, by Dr. Raymond Moody, reports of the phenomenon go back many years before Moody began researching them. It would be difficult to find a more profound NDE than that reported by Cora L. V. Richmond in her 1923 book entitled *My Experiences While Out of My Body*. "The possibility of the spirit 'leaving the body' for a time and then returning to its usual activities has been demonstrated many times," she wrote more than 50 years before Moody's classic book *Life After Life*, going on to point out that the separation can be caused by accident or illness but sometimes by "voluntary absence," referred to as simply an out-of-body experience (OBE).

"These visits to 'heaven'," she continued, "would be sometimes tinged with the religious bias of the subject, but this is not strange in view of the fact that spirit states are conditions of the mind and spirits experiencing them." Nearly a century later, skeptical scientists are making this same observation as if it is something new and offering it as evidence that the experience is nothing more than a hallucination.

In addition to several NDEs, Richmond seems to have been adept at departing her body voluntarily. It is not entirely clear from her book, but the primary experience reported on appears to have come during a serious illness, when she was near death for a number of days, several years before her actual death at age 82, in 1923, However, she claimed to have had many out-of-body experiences and it is sometimes difficult to discern if everything she reports in the book resulted from that one NDE during her serious illness or whether some of it came from other experiences.

She begins the book by stating that it is impossible to adequately convey in human language what she actually experienced, especially in the higher states of the afterlife environment, and that the best she could do was make an attempt at offering some glimpses of her experience. She recalled a great sense of relief – of being set free from the limitations of the body and did not expect to return to it as she had previously done.

"There was a perception of great Light, a consciousness of Illumination, an awakening to the vastness, the unlimitation of this Realm of Spirit," she explained. "All else was swallowed up – eclipsed by the wonderful experiences that came – the Beloved Presences – the vistas of luminous Spirits! This was a state of Super-Consciousness; the awakening of faculties and perceptions before unknown, of being aware, almost without limitation; of KNOWING! Whatever is the nature and state of the real Ego this seemed as near to the Absolute as one could well conceive! There was so much of me! There was so little of me! There were so many and such surpassing spirits! How one shrinks in the presences of the mighty ones! How one expands in the Knowledge of the Infinite: His Image!"

Deceased loved ones welcomed her. "The Best Beloved, those who had preceded me into this wondrous life, came thronging around, by degrees," she wrote, "to welcome me:

not all at once, but first those who were by tenderest ties the nearest and the dearest." She learned that spirits of kindred thoughts, perceptions, and aspirations are attracted to each other and form groups who work together for others. "I saw them 'moving upon' the minds of those in Earth-forms whom they could reach, sometimes singly, sometimes in groups, as the conditions might require."

Her guide took her on a tour of the spirit world. She witnessed scenes in which spirits were attempting to minister to those humans under their guidance but failed because of earthly barriers, primarily selfishness and not being open to spirit influence due to false education, both theological and material. She saw those recently deceased and not yet fully awakened to their new state existing in the thought-forms and scenes of their recent earthly lives as they lacked the spiritual awareness to fully recognize and appreciate their new states. "As the Spirit unfolds, the thought-forms change and then disappear as perception takes the place of limitation by the senses," it was explained to her. Many of those reproducing familiar scenes of their earth conditions seemed satisfied, some even happy, "not even knowing that this similitude was the result of their own thought-forms instead of being inherent or organic in the 'spirit land'." But, there were many others whose thought-forms were of the "shadowed kind" and apparently not especially pleasant.

More Awareness

Richmond went on to say that she became more and more aware that she could perceive and receive more perfectly the answer to every question, even before its formulation in thought. "Formulation is a process of limitation, sometimes of hindrance," her spirit guide told her, explaining that prepared senses are the result of prepared minds; that is, minds prepared by the awareness of spirit while in the material life.

She prayed that she would not have to return to her physical body, but her guide informed her that she still had work to do and must return. She was taken by her guide to view her body and observed it still breathing while also seeing a "psychic cord" connecting her spirit form to it. The guide told her that although she would not immediately return to her body, that it was necessary for her to keep her spirit *"en rapport"* with the body. Thus, during the experience over "many days" of earth time she was required to return to the body to keep the "vital spark" alive. She likened the idea of returning to visiting dear friends in a place of beauty and enchantment and then having to return to one's daily routine.

She was taken by her guide to witness those "working with themselves." One such soul she recognized as a person who had been considered "eminent" in the art world while in the material life. He was cutting, carving, and breathing upon an image of himself. She asked the guide what the man was doing. "Removing the angularities and errors of his own nature: jealously of other artists, the deepest scar; selfish love of human praise – that overweening desire for adulation; unwillingness to accord to others the appreciation of their true merits," the guide explained.

"Spirit states are as varied as are the personal states of those composing them," Richmond observed. "The knowledge – or lack of it – possessed by the person IS the spirit state, i.e., knowledge of spiritual principles." In effect, the more we come to understand relative to spiritual principles in the earth life, the better off we are after transitioning to the spirit world, assuming that we live by those principles. "Time does not seem to be a factor in the realm of spirits except as related to people and events in the human state with which spirits have connection," she further explained. "Our human phrases, and even our usual thoughts seem superficial, weak, and puerile when endeavoring to describe the divine realities of the Spirit."

Her tour of the higher or more celestial realms was completely beyond description. "No human language is in the smallest degree adequate to portray the ecstasy produced by the vision, contemplation of perception of this all-glorious state," she went on. "Orb on orb of transcendent beauty, sphere on sphere of celestial splendor!." And while spirits in those higher realms were more unified in purpose, they retained their individuality. "This Individuality is Eternal; is the Ego of which the small personality of earth and even of the spirit states is but a fragment of manifestation."

Richmond asked her guide why knowledge of the spirit world is not made more available to humans and was told that it was a matter of growth, unfoldment, waiting and working. In other words, most people are not yet ready for it.

In concluding the book, Richmond mentioned that some eminent men of science had made headway in helping humans understand the future life. She named Hare, Mapes, Denton, Wallace, Crookes, Varley, Zollner, and Flammarion, but she placed Sir Oliver Lodge, an esteemed British physicist, at the top of the list, as one whose mind was best prepared to receive spiritual truths.

There is so much more to the story of Cora L. V. Richmond than her NDEs and OBEs. She was perhaps the most amazing medium of the nineteenth century, possibly the greatest medium in 2000 years. Beginning in 1851, at age 11, as Cora Scott, she would go into a trance state and vacate her body, permitting various advanced spirits to speak through her vocal cords, lecturing to thousands of people in the United States and England on various subjects pertaining to their spiritual welfare, including philosophical, social, political, and reform matters.

8

The Physician Who
Watched Himself Die

~

I n his 1903 book, *Human Personality and Its Survival of Bodily Death* (published two years after his death in 1901), Frederic W. H. Myers, the pioneering psychical researcher, set forth a story about what is now known as a near-death experience, which took place in 1889. It was told to him by Dr. A. S. Wiltse, a physician of Skiddy, Kansas, known to both Myers and fellow researcher, Dr. Richard Hodgson, as a "careful and conscientious witness."

Wiltse was suffering from typhoid fever. "I passed about four hours in all without pulse or perceptible heartbeat, as I am informed by Dr. S. H. Raynes, who was the only physician present," Wiltse related in a letter to Myers. "During a portion of this time several of the bystanders thought I was dead, and such a report being carried outside, the village church bell was tolled. Dr. Raynes informs me, however, that by bringing his eyes close to my face, he could perceive an occasional short gasp, so very light as to be barely perceptible, and that he was upon the point, several times of saying, 'He is dead,' when a gasp would occur in time to check him."

Raynes pricked Wiltse with a needle at various points on his body but got no response. It was later estimated that while Wiltse was without pulse for about four hours, his state of "apparent death" lasted only about half-an-hour. "I lost, I believe, all power of thought or knowledge of existence in absolute unconsciousness," Wiltse continued the story. "I came again into a state of conscious existence and discovered that I was still in the body, but the body and I had no longer any interest in common. I looked in astonishment and joy for the first time upon myself – the me, the real Ego, while the not-me closed it upon all side like a sepulcher of clay.

"With all the interest of a physician, I beheld the wonders of my bodily anatomy, intimately interwoven with which, even tissue for tissue, was I, the living soul of that dead body. I learned that the epidermis was the outside boundary of the ultimate tissues, so to speak, of the soul. I realized my condition and reasoned calmly thus. I have died, as men term death, and yet I am as much a man as ever. I am about to get out of the body. I watched the interesting process of the separation of soul and body. By some power, apparently not my own, the Ego was rocked to and fro, laterally, as a cradle is rocked, by which process its connection with the tissues of the body was broken up. After a little time the lateral motion ceased, and long the soles of the feet beginning at the toes, passing rapidly to the heels, I felt and heard, as it seemed, the snapping of innumerable small cords. When this was accomplished, I began slowly to retreat from the feet, toward the head, as a rubber cord shortens. I remember reaching the hips and saying to myself, 'Now, there is no life below the hips.'"

Dr. Wiltse could not recall passing through the abdomen or chest, but he recollected that his "whole self" was collected into his head. He appeared to himself something like a jellyfish in color and form and remembered thinking that he would soon be free. As "he" emerged from his head, he saw two women sitting at the head of his physical shell and wondered if there was room for him to stand.

Floating Up & Down

"As I emerged from the head, I floated up and down and laterally like a soap bubble attached to the bowl of a pipe until I at last broke loose from the body and fell lightly to the floor, where I slowly arose and expanded into the full stature of a man. I seemed to be translucent, of a bluish cast and perfectly naked. With a painful sense of embarrassment, I fled toward the partially opened door to escape the eyes of the two ladies whom I was facing, as well as others who I knew were about me, but upon reaching the door I found myself clothed, and satisfied upon that point, I turned and faced the company."

To Wiltse's surprise, the arm of one man standing near the door passed through his arm without resistance. The man gave no sign of the contact or of seeing Wiltse as he continued to gaze toward the couch. "I directed my gaze in the direction of his and saw my own dead body."

Wiltse recalled being surprised at how pale the body looked but congratulated himself on the way he had composed his body, his hands clasped at his chest. He saw the two women weeping, but, at the time, did not recognize them as his wife and sister, as he had no conception of individuality. He then attempted to gain the attention of the people gathered in the room, but he was unsuccessful.

"It did not once occur to me to speak, and I concluded the matter by saying to myself; 'They see only with the eyes of the body. They cannot see spirits. They are watching what they think is I, but they are mistaken. That is not I. This is I and I am as much alive as ever.'

Since no one was paying any attention to the real "him," Wiltse wandered outside. "I never saw the street more distinctly than I saw it then," he continued. "I took note of the redness of the soil and of the washes the rain had made. I took a rather pathetic look about me, like one who is about to leave his home for a long time. Then I discovered that I had become larger than I was in earth life and congratulated myself thereupon. I was somewhat smaller in the body than I just liked to be, but in the next life, I thought, I am to be as I desired."

Wiltse marveled at how well he was feeling, when only minutes before he was in extreme distress. He then looked back through the open door, where he could see his body. "I discovered then a small cord, like a spider's web, running from my shoulders (of the spirit body) back to my body and attaching to it at the base of my neck in front."

Some Vast Intelligence

He soon became aware of a "presence," which he could not see, but which he knew was entering into an overhead cloud form the southern side. "The presence did not seem, to my mind, as a form, because it filled the cloud like some vast intelligence… Then from the right side and from the left of the cloud a tongue of black vapor shot forth and rested lightly upon either side of my head, and as they touched me thoughts not my own entered into my brain. "These, I said, are his thoughts and not mine; they might be in Greek or Hebrew for all power I have over them. But how kindly am I addressed in my mother tongue that so I may understand all his will. Yet, although the language was English, it was so eminently above my power to reproduce that my rendition of it is far short of the original. The following is as near as I can render it:

"This is the road to the eternal world. Yonder rocks are the boundary between the two worlds and the two lives. Once you pass them, you can no more return into the body. If your work is complete on earth, you may pass beyond the rocks. If, however, upon consideration you conclude that…it is not done, you can return into the body."

Wiltse approached the rocks. "I was tempted to cross the boundary line. I hesitated and reasoned thus: 'I have died once and if I go back, soon or late, I must die again. If I stay someone else will do my work, and so the end will be as well and as surely accomplished, and shall I die again? I will not, but now that I am so near I will cross the line and stay."

But as he attempted to cross the line, a black cloud appeared in front of him. "I knew that I was to be stopped. I felt the power to move or to think leaving me. My hands fell powerless at my side, my head dropped forward, the cloud touched my face and I knew no more." In "astonishment and disappointment," Wiltse then found himself back in his physical body. "What in the world has happened to me? he exclaimed. "Must I die again?"

9

Sort of a Cloud but Not a Cloud

◠

"What are we to make of it?"

That question was put to members of the Royal Medical Society by Sir Auckland Geddes, a British surgeon turned statesman, at the Society's bicentenary celebration in 1937. Sir Auckland was referring to the strange experience of a man who had seemingly "died" and then returned with a detailed memory of all he had seen and done. The "near-death experience" phenomenon, which strongly suggests a spirit or etheric body in addition the physical body, was for the most part unheard of then.

Sir Auckland explained that while the man (the experiencer) wished to remain anonymous, he had no doubt as to the man's credibility. "Of one thing only can we be quite sure," he said. "It is not a fake. Without certainty of this I should not have brought it to your notice." Although uncertain, it might be inferred from Sir Auckland's preliminary comments that that the experiencer was another physician, but there was also speculation that it was Sir Auckland himself.

The complete account of the NDE was read by Sir Auckland and was recorded in the Scotsman and in the June 1937 issue of *The Edinburgh Medical Journal*.

The experiencer reported that on November 9th, a few minutes after midnight, he began to feel very ill. By 2 a.m., he realized he was suffering from acute gastro-enteritis, which kept him vomiting and purging until about 8 a.m. By 10 a.m., he concluded that he had developed all the symptoms of a very acute poisoning, including intense gastro-intestinal pain, diarrhea, and with "pulse and respiration quite impossible to count." He wanted to ring for assistance, but could not. Realizing that he was very ill, he quickly reviewed his financial position.

Separation of Consciousness

"...at no time did my consciousness appear to me to be in any way dimmed, but I suddenly realized that my consciousness was separating from another consciousness, which was also me," the experiencer reported. "These for purposes of description we could call the A and B consciousness, and throughout what follows, the ego attached itself to the A consciousness."

The experiencer recognized that the B personality belonged to the body. As his condition grew worse, he noticed that his heart was fibrillating rather than beating. "I realized that the B consciousness belonging to the body was beginning to show signs of becoming composite, that is, built up of 'consciousness' from the head, the heart, the viscera & c.

"These components became more individual, and the B consciousness began to disintegrate, while the A consciousness which was now me, seemed to be altogether outside my body, which it could see. Gradually I realized that I could see not only my body and the bed in which it was, but everything in the whole house and garden, and then I realized that I was seeing not only 'things' at home, but in London and Scotland, in fact wherever my attention was directed it seemed to me; and the explanation which I received, from what source I do not know, but which I found myself calling to myself my mentor, was that I was free in a time dimension of space, wherein 'now' was in some way equivalent to 'here' in the ordinary three-dimension space of everyday life."

Four Dimensional

The experiencer then realized that his vision included not only "things" in the ordinary three-dimensional world, but also "things" in the four or more dimensional places in which he found himself.

"From now on the description is and must be entirely metaphorical," he continued, "because there are no words which really describe what I saw, or rather appreciated. Although I had no body, I had what appeared to be perfect two-eyed vision, and what I saw can only be described in this way, that I was conscious of a psychic stream flowing with life through time, and this gave me the impression of being visible, and it seemed to me to have particularly intense iridescence. I understood from my mentor that all our brains are just end organs projecting as it were from the three-dimensional universe into the psychic stream, and flowing with it into the fourth and fifth dimensions."

Around each brain, as the experiencer saw it, there seemed to be a condensation of the psychic stream, which appeared as a small cloud. "While I was just appreciating this, the mentor who was conveying information to me explained that the fourth dimension was in everything existing in the three-dimensional space, and at the same time everything in the three-dimensional space existed in the fourth dimension, and also in the fifth dimension, and I at the time quite clearly understood what was meant, and quite understood how 'now' in the fourth-dimensional universe was just the same to all intents and purposes as 'here' in a three-dimensional view of things.

"I then realized that I myself was a condensation, as it were, in the psychic stream, a sort of cloud that was not a cloud, and the visual impression I had of myself was blue." Gradually, the experiencer began to recognize a number of people he knew and saw the "psychic condensation" attached to them. He also saw a number of people who had very little psychic condensation attached to them. He saw different colors – blue, purple and dark red, pink, grey-brown, pearly, apricot, and brown around various acquaintances. As he was observing all of this, he saw the woman with the purple and dark red condensation enter the room and hurry to the telephone to call his doctor.

Upon his initial examination, the treating physician commented, "He is nearly gone." The experiencer heard him clearly speaking to him on the bed, but could not reply. "I was really cross when he took a syringe and rapidly injected my body with something which I afterwards learned was camphor," the experiencer continued his account. "As the heart began to beat more strongly, I was drawn back, and I was intensely annoyed, because I was so interested, and just beginning to understand where I was and what I was 'seeing.' I came back into the body really angry at being pulled back, and once I was back all the clarity of vision of anything and everything disappeared, and I was just possessed of a glimmer of consciousness which was suffused with pain."

The experiencer went on to say that the "dream, vision, or experience has shown no tendency to fade like a dream would fade, nor has it shown any tendency that I am aware of to grow or to rationalize itself as a dream would do." Further, he had had no repetition of any sort or kind of the experience of clear understanding that he had experienced while "free from the body."

Indeed, what are we to make of it?

10

The Most Dynamic NDE
You'll Ever Read About

~

In her 1917 book, *How I Know that the Dead Are Alive,* Fanny Ruthven Paget offers one of the most vivid and detailed near-death experiences ever recorded. While not clearly stating her illness, one might infer that Paget, a resident of Houston, Texas, suffered from severe pneumonia for several days during 1911.

"All about and above me I could see nothing, but fancy my astonishment if you can, when looking down, I saw my body resting peacefully on the bed, representing what is commonly called a 'dead person,'" Paget recalled. "I could not move my eyes from it; it fascinated me as it lay in the cold whiteness, robed in a gown of lavender silk, with dainty laces and ruffles... The deep blue 'windows of the soul,' the eyes, were at half-mast; the soul being absent the light was gone; the lips slightly parted wore just a suggestion of a smile; the left hand rested lightly on the breast – the engagement ring scintillating as brightly as ever; the right, which no doubt had been lifted unconsciously at the shock of impact, had fallen a little apart from the body and lay, palm upturned. How peaceful it looked!

"Thus every detail of the clay image fastened itself upon my consideration as I viewed it dispassionately, realizing that it was a cast-off garment for which I had no further use. However, I felt a protective kindliness toward it; it had been a faithful servant, executing my every wish and whim and now that I had passed beyond the range of its services, it pleased my fancy to robe it in the white, pearl-be-decked dress, the wearing of which had meant so much to me in quite a different way."

Paget then concerned herself with her fiancé in another town and found herself being propelled by a vibratory sensation to his sleeping body. "As I looked upon him I saw the shadow body more distinctly than the physical. Viewed from the other side of life, the 'shadow' body seemed the original and the physical the duplicate, the soul the real, the body the unreal. Within and interpenetrating all was a light, which I had not before perceived as being a part of the spiritual anatomy. This light penetrated from within, both the shadow and physical bodies, maintaining through and about the body an aura or illumination which enveloped it; clothing it, as it were, in a magnetized illumination. How wonderful this three-in-one life-manifestation seemed, especially when we generally recognize only the one – the physical!"

Talking to the Living

Moving closer to her fiancé, Paget attempted to converse with him, but he slept on, even though his soul, which was not sleeping, responded joyously and tried to help her penetrate his physical consciousness as he moaned and turned restlessly in his sleep. After a few moments, he cried out, "Fanny, Fanny," and sat up in bed, wide awake. As he turned on a light and reached for his glasses and a magazine, she tried to communicate, but he did not react to her words. "I am dead, that is why he cannot hear and see me," she thought, further recalling that she felt more alive than she had ever felt. "There was something pitiably painful about being so near one beloved, seeing him plainly and hearing him distinctly, even knowing that he was thinking of me, and yet having him utterly ignore my presence, and above all knowing that he would never recognize me again – never hear my voice no matter how ardently I called, while I was the same in every way minus the physical body."

Then she perceived that her vibratory environment did not harmonize with his. "Mine was the vibration of perpetual motion – his more like a 'dead sea' into which these vibratory currents ebbed and flowed, and it seemed such an easy matter to move out of the 'deadness' into the 'ebb and flow' that I waited and watched a long time before I realized that he would make no effort to do so."

Realizing that she would not be able to penetrate his physical consciousness, she bade him farewell and attempted to move on; however, the vibratory force seemed to restrain her. "Persistently the force held me, as though inviting me to further considerations of earth interests, but I had none. My material possessions were disposed of as I desired; there was no life-work I was leaving incomplete; I had no children, no one depending on me; nothing held me to the earth. My desire had been to go beyond it and now that I had done so, I was well pleased and wanted to go on to the joys I felt awaited me beyond the influence of earth. Yet the force held me, try as I would to pass beyond it, until, instead of struggling against it I tried to understand it – to wrest from it its reason for thus detaining me, feeling that there must be some reason for such marked persistence. Almost instantly the lesson sank into my consciousness and I realized that the long arm of mundane interests can reach into the Beyond and hold its victims within the shadow of earth – pitting its magnetism against the promise of higher things."

She then felt herself moving in an undulating way within the propelling vibration and was suddenly enveloped in oppressive heavy darkness, feeling alone in eternity and waiting in awesome uncertainty. She perceived that the darkness was really within her and could be eliminated only from within. "There were loved ones and many others welcoming me and rejoicing that I was with them." Her spirit guide, who identified himself as Meon, was also there. She now felt light and carefree.

Visiting "Hell"

Meon then told her to follow him, "and with a soft, bluish light playing about and enveloping us, we floated out on the undulating waves of space." As they were propelled by vibratory waves, they encountered a "red darkness" where she found herself among many others. "I was listening, trying to hear what they were saying but the vibrations were evidently not in harmony, so I could not hear distinctly, and after a long time of vain effort I turned to Meon, and asked 'What place is this?'" Meon explained that they were in a place still very much within earth's magnetism, or spiritual gravitation. Paget asked why the souls were detained there and Meon informed her that some desire it while others were not yet strong enough to progress beyond that point. "Earth interests hold them," he explained.

"There was no bar to their going on but they did not want to; some did not know they could not give up the earth life," Paget related. "In this dark earth-magnetized region disembodied spirits lived the mundane existence much as the psychic lives the spiritual while yet in the mundane – one in progression, the other retrogression. Disembodied spirits living the mundane life do so at the expense of human beings in the earth life, while the mundane person living the spiritual life is obeying the law of evolution and progression."

Paget observed spirits of love and mercy attempting to help those souls stuck in this "hellish" realm, but most of them had not yet acquired "spiritual hearing" and did not respond to the offers of assistance. There were some, however, who heard and struggled up from the vortex. Meon informed her that no soul was irretrievably lost, no matter how many eons it may remain in the darkness.

Paget began to wonder if this was to be her new abode, but Meon assured her that it was not. "Did not the Christ descend into this place before his ascension?" he addressed her concern.

"Far out beyond the red-fringed darkness I could see light, in which rainbows seemed to play, pale as the dawn, of a gray-weird loveliness, coming and going as though flirting with the darkness, for to embrace it would be to destroy," she continued on. "For delicate beauty it seemed I had never seen anything more fascinating or alluring than this kiss of the dawn and the darkness in the Soul world – it was like kissing death goodbye."

The Dawn World

They passed into what seemed to be another world. Paget called it the "Dawn World," since it seemed that the light began to neutralize the darkness. "There were houses, flowers, trees, everything was so life-like it amazed me. I almost fancied I had returned to earth." The inhabitants conversed with her, but they did not seem to realize that they were in the "after life," as they were not entirely free of earth's magnetism. Paget witnessed some of them going earthward, as though drawn by something of paramount importance. "While there seemed no doubt that these people once inhabited the earth, I saw no one I had ever known in this life. They had possibly progressed there out of the darkness and would go back to help those less fortunate into the higher condition which they had attained."

Meon and Paget vibrated onward in ever increasing light. "So enchanting was this riding on vibratory waves of space in a gentle undulatory way, that I felt like going on forever, and forever, never tiring, never stopping, but after abandoning myself to the witchery of it for some time, I perceived the vibrations changing, merging into a quivering sensation, even more exquisite, and then, as if part of it, my feet came upon something different, something firm and reliable."

She now found herself in a city of light, one of whiteness, boundless in expanse. "It seemed I had reached the limit of my ability to float in space. It seemed that I was heavier than my surroundings in some way. Everywhere were the most exalted souls I had yet seen. Some came forward and greeted us, addressing Meon as though he were one of them, and then, together, we entered into a building immeasurable in space and height, the veritable soul of architectural magnificence. The material had the transparency of glass of a variegated whiteness, into which colors, harmonizing in the most delicate way, were coming and going, ever changing. Electricity seemed to be the power which held it all together, as the electric blue would merge into violet and play incessantly, in a serpentine way, into which almost imperceptible yellowish streams seemed to flow. It was self-illuminated...It seemed that all the wisdom of all the ages was mine as I stood there. Life and death gave up their mysteries, and I no longer wondered but observed as one who understood. The machinery of earth existence was operated and regulated by and through the power of this plane. It was actually in contact with the earth. No happening on earth escaped the observation of the great spirits who seemed to have nothing else to do but watch over the beings of earth, to teach them, to lift them up through darkness, watch over reincarnations, create teachers and place them where they were most needed. With these teachers they were in direct communication at all times and knew exactly what was going on through some form of wireless telegraphy or telephony, perhaps, but they communicated as though there were no distance.

"They seemed to draw the highly evolved souls of earth up to them mentally, and these cooperated consciously, responding unerringly. It was marvelous to watch the process or rather processes, as there were many phases of this supervision. There were coming and going all the time. I saw many go out and disappear into the depths, all rejoicing in their work, the uplifting of humanity. The souls were countless, the space immeasurable, yet there was no confusion – it was system idealized, each recognizing his mission and doing it. Truly, it was the Christ principle manifested, for they were laboring for others, not themselves."

Meon took Paget even higher, where the influence of earth was not felt. A great soul came forward and asked her if she would like to return to earth. She said she would like to return only if she could do good by telling others what she had experienced. The being warned her that many would not believe her and that she might suffer from her efforts, but Paget said she was up for the challenge.

A Life Review

Paget then felt alone with bowed head. She then saw a little light vibrating directly before her. It began shaping itself into something. "It was not unlike a moving picture." She began to see figures and a small girl emerged. She soon realized that the young girl was herself and she was reliving her life on earth. She saw herself reveling in her grand passion, music, which held her in bondage as she grew in the joy and mastery of it. "How the little, white fingers, too small to span an octave, subconsciously caught fragments from the 'choir invisible' and imprisoned them on the piano!

She saw herself grow through college and into a proud, self-centered woman. There appeared before her three roads, one labeled "Good," one "Evil," and the other, the center, was unlabeled. She found herself on the center road, which had many more people than either of the side roads. "These roads were guarded by invisible creatures, according to the indicated propensities of each, who were always calling to those who traveled in the center, in an endeavor to influence them to more determined tendencies. Ever and anon there were paths leading from the center to the outer roads and from one outer road to the other, showing how easily one can change ones course at will."

Paget then saw the young woman dreaming of becoming a great singer, the compensation being the homage of the world. "I saw her holding to heart in enchanted fancy, as the only thing worthwhile, the emptiest of all life's coveted cups – Fame." There was no one to remind her that 'by ambition fell the angels."

The "movie" of her life continued on to the time she came down with a severe case of laryngitis and lost her singing voice. She saw herself cursing God and being enveloped by a shadow-stained covering of materialism. She saw both her parents pass into the spirit world, leaving her alone, fighting the bitter fight. She saw even the most trivial matters in her life review. "Its faithfulness to detail was perfectly marvelous. Nothing was hidden, nothing slurred over. It was *all* there. I was standing face to face with my earth life just as I had lived it, awaiting its condemnation or justification."

When the life review ended, Meon stood waiting. He told her that the purpose of the review was to build an edifice on the ashes as she returned to earth life.

'Meon and other spirits were hovering about me. I could feel the electrified essence, which had manifested its presence everywhere during my voyage, drawing itself away – letting me go, as it were. Then the burden of physical life was full upon me and what a misfit I was!'

11

An Intriguing 1911
Near-Death Experience

~

February 24, 2014

The *Sunday Express* of May 26, 1935 carried an account of what today would be called a near-death experience by Mr. W. Martin of Liverpool, England. Martin wrote: "In 1911, at the age of sixteen, I was staying about twelve miles away from my own house when a high wall was blown down by a sudden gust of wind as I was passing. A huge coping stone hit me on top of my head.

"It then seemed as if I could see myself lying on the ground, huddled up, with one corner of the stone resting on my head and quite a number of people rushing toward me. I watched them move the stone and someone took off his coat and put it under my head, and I heard all their comments. 'Fetch a doctor.' 'His neck is broken.' 'Skull smashed!'

"He then wanted to know if anyone knew where I lived, and on being told I was lodging just around the corner, he instructed them to carry me there.

"Now all this time it appeared as though I were disembodied from the form lying on the ground and suspended in midair in the center of the group, and I could hear everything that was being said.

"As they started to carry me it was remarked that it would come as a blow to my people, and I was immediately conscious of a desire to be with my mother. Instantly I was at home, and father and mother were just sitting down to their midday meal. On my entrance mother sat bolt upright in her chair and said, 'Bert, something has happened to our boy.'

"There followed an argument, but my mother refused to be pacified, and said that if she caught the 2 p.m. train she could be with me before three.

"She had hardly left the room when there came a knock at the front door. It was a porter from the railway station with a telegram saying I was badly hurt.

"Then suddenly I was again transported – this time it seemed to be against my will – to a bedroom where a woman whom I recognized was in bed, and two other women were quietly bustling around, and a doctor was leaning over the bed. Then the doctor had a baby in his hands. At once I became aware of an almost irresistible impulse to press my face through the back of the baby's head so that my face would come out at the same place as the child's.

"The doctor said, 'It looks as though we have lost them both,' and again, I felt the urge to take the baby's place to show him he was wrong, but the thoughts of my mother crying turned my thoughts in her direction, when straightaway I was in a railway carriage with her and my father.

"I was still with them when they arrived at my lodging and were shown into my room where I had been put to bed. Mother was beside the bed and I longed to comfort her, and the realization came that I ought to do the same thing I had felt impelled to do in the case of the baby and climb into the body on the bed.

"At last I succeeded, and the effort caused the real me to sit up in bed fully conscious. Mother made me lie down again, but

I said that I was all right, and remarked that it was odd that she knew something was wrong before the porter had brought the telegram.

"Both she and Dad were amazed at my knowledge. Their astonishment was further increased when I repeated almost word for word some of the conversation they had had at home and in the train. I said that I had been close to birth as well as death, and told them that Mrs. Wilson, who lived close to us at home, had had a baby that day, but it was dead because I would not get into its body We subsequently learned that Mrs. Wilson died on the same day at 2:05 p.m. after delivering a stillborn girl."

Part III

The NDE in Recent Times

"It's remarkable how [survival] research has been for the most part ignored by religion, but frankly, I'm relieved."
—**Gary E. Schwartz**, Ph.D.

12

A Science Professor Sees the Light

〜

When he went out for a run one day in 1983, Dr. Donald Morse, a Temple University science professor, was like many of his scientific colleagues, not believing in anything beyond the material world. His views regarding a spiritual world and life after death began to change a few minutes into his workout.

As Morse exercised, things started spinning around in ever widening circles and everything began slowing down. His heart was racing and was so loud that he thought it would burst through his chest. Then it began to slow down and seemed to stop completely. He then fell to the ground. "I knew I was dying, but I wasn't afraid," recalls Morse, a 71-year-old resident of Cherry Hill, New Jersey, now retired. "The light was incredibly beautiful, and I felt wonderfully calm and secure with a benevolent presence beside me."

Morse describes the light as being extremely bright and white. "It enveloped me so that I could see nothing but this light. I was not afraid. I felt secure, warm, and serene." He then recalls seeing his whole life flash before him, including temper tantrums as a child, his victory in a dart-throwing contest, a hospital bout with colitis, asthma attacks, family visits, throwing a player out at home plate, shooting a winning basket, crying when the New York Giants lost a game, seeing his father die from lung cancer, getting married, seeing his three children born, doing a surgical procedure on the day President Kennedy was killed, receiving a Temple University research award, as well as many other events in his life.

When the life review ended, he remembers leaving his body, flying over the clouds, and arriving at Mt. Eden Cemetery in Valhalla, New York, where he observed his funeral...or what might have been his funeral had he decided not to return to his body. He recalls reading his obituary in the paper the next day. Shortly thereafter, he felt the sharp pain of an injection and realized he was still in the hospital.

Morse had taken his run on the grounds of a large Philadelphia hospital, where he had been hospitalized after suffering a severe reaction to quinacrine, a drug used to treat a gastrointestinal disease. However, he felt strong enough that day to get in a little light exercise. Apparently, he wasn't strong enough. While Morse now understands that he was having a near-death experience, he didn't recognize it as such then. "I was a research scientist who was well schooled in evolutionary biology, genetics, microbiology, immunology, and with some knowledge of archaeology, anthropology, cosmology, and quantum physics," he muses. "At that time I had never heard of an NDE. I was an agnostic and considered it a hallucination. I pushed it to the back of my mind, although I'd often think about it."

Anxiety Problems

In 1995, following the death of his sister and some friends and relatives, Morse began suffering from a "general anxiety disorder" relating to his own mortality. He couldn't concentrate, couldn't sleep, couldn't exercise, couldn't enjoy his food, and began experiencing abdominal cramps and neuralgic-like headaches. It was then that he began to try and make sense out of his NDE. "Even though I didn't see the spiritual connection at first, the NDE did trigger a tremendous change in me," Morse offers.

"Those 12 years between the NDE and the death anxiety were the most productive of my life. I could go to a lecture and be writing something on a tablet totally unrelated to what was being discussed, but I'd still know what was being talked about in the lecture. I could deal with all kinds of distractions that previously bothered me. From what I've read, that happens to a lot of people who have had NDEs. There's something going on in the subconscious, both physically and psychologically."

Morse began reading everything he could about near-death-experiences, out-of-body travel, apparitions, visions, dreams, spirit communication, the occult, past-life regressions, psychic phenomena, the paranormal, life after death, spiritual evolution, God and the universe, and found a preponderance of evidence that allowed him to formulate a rational depiction of the afterlife. His findings and views are now set forth in a book, *Searching for Eternity* (Eagle Wing Books, Inc., 2000)

Although some of his scientific colleagues may feel that Morse has "abandoned ship," Morse says that he still believes in the scientific laws and principles he had learned and followed over his 45-year scientific career. "It's just with the one law that science cannot and might never understand," he continues. "That is the law that explains where we came from. In a nutshell, I cannot comprehend a universe that is intelligent enough to create itself with all of the million-to-one incredibly chance phenomena that eventually resulted in an intelligent human species. In addition, I cannot believe that 16 million people who have had near-death experiences, which mimic many of the great religions' concepts of the afterlife, could have created it in their brains."

Morse agrees with the eminent Swiss psychiatrist, Carl Jung, that death is man's greatest fear, especially in the second half of life. "Some people can suppress it, repress it, or deny it better than others," he explains. "But we all have it. Some people go through life at a fantastic pace just to block out their thoughts on death." To overcome this death anxiety, Morse advocates a holistic, integrative approach to stress management. That involves cultivating an awareness of death, grasping the fact that the consciousness does survive, and that death is merely a transition to another realm of existence.

"The more you learn about it," he says, "the more you understand it and face it without too much stress or anxiety."

13

The Man Who Fell Off Everest

~

October 26, 2020

A friend recently asked me to identify the most interesting near-death experience (NDE) I have heard or read about. I told him that I couldn't do that without considerable thought, but one that immediately came to mind and would certainly be among those at the top of the list was that of Roger Hart, a retired geophysicist. His NDE took place on May 29, 1962, at age 21, when he was part of an American team attempting to climb Mount Everest.

I had the opportunity to interview Hart in Newport, Oregon shortly after the release of his 2003 book *The Phaselock Code*, subtitled *Through Time, Death, and Reality, the Metaphysical Adventures of the Man Who Fell off Everest*.

As captain of the cross-country team at Tufts University, Hart had just won a race against Amherst when he met Woody Sayre, a Tufts philosophy professor. The two became friends and shared an interest in rock climbing. Some months after their first meeting, Sayre asked Hart to be part of a team that would attempt to climb Mt. Everest without the use of supplemental oxygen.

During that climb, a crampon gave way and Hart and Sayre fell about 180 feet down a snowy cliff. Hart recalled stars rushing by him like tracer bullets as he yelled and screamed. As soon as he thought that he was about to die, his soul ripped free. As described in the book, he shot off into starless space, floated free in gravity, and watched his body, as if in slow motion, tumble over the ice cliffs below. "I perched on the cusp of time, where, like a water drop between watersheds, I could choose between worlds."

Hart further recalled a great warmth and euphoria overtaking him and feeling wonderful that he was about to die. "I could see in all directions at once, not with the seeing of eyes but the seeing of dreams. I felt no fear and no cold; space seemed to shrink around me, or perhaps I expanded to it. At any rate, I was no longer afraid of the emptiness below me." He remembers thinking, *Here you are about to die and you feel wonderful – you are so weird!*

Although it was thought to be impossible for humans to survive a night of sub-zero temperatures without a tent, Hart and Sayre endured the night huddled together with a nylon tent shell wrapped around them. The ledge on which they had landed was too narrow to pitch a tent.

Before the experience, Hart equated being alive with material success, having control of as many possessions as possible. "I did not believe anything unless I actually experienced it or could prove it scientifically, as with electromagnetic radiation, quantum mechanics, or relativity," explained Hart, who was a research professor at the Oregon State College school of Ocean and Atmospheric Sciences before his retirement. The fall, even though it took only a few seconds as we know it, changed Hart's ideas in that regard, convincing him that there is life after death and that spiritual intelligence guides the universe. "Before the NDE on Everest, I was a rationalist, reductive materialist and skeptic. I believed matter was the basis of life and by reducing matter to its smallest components we could understand the universe according to predetermined laws of physics."

His graduate studies at Yale became meaningless to him and he was appalled by the greed and ambition of his fellow graduate students. However, two of his Yale classes – quantum mechanics and statistical thermodynamics – helped him understand the experience. The pioneering NDE research of Drs. Raymond Moody and Elisabeth Kübler-Ross had not yet taken place and therefore Hart could not make any sense out of the experience. It stayed with him and "grew like a sprouting seed in my psyche."

Since my interview with Hart was more than 40 years after his experience, I asked him how much detail he actually remembered. "I have strong memories of the mental aspects," he responded. "In addition, since the feeling during the NDE was so extraordinary, I've meditated on it, relived it so to speak, over the course of the past 40 years." He added that beginning with Moody's *Life After Life*, he's been able to compare his experience with those of others. "There are some similarities but many differences. I felt elation, time dilation, and separation of mind from body, but I don't recall going through a tunnel, doing a life review, or meeting with loved ones in the afterlife. I think the important thing in my case was that I abandoned the normal internal dialogue and much of the normal information processing. That allowed, momentarily, a reality free of time and interconnected with other parts of the universe, full of light with an extraordinary feeling of bliss. I believe the NDE opened new neural pathways and enabled access to a higher mind function with connections to the universal field of information."

Second NDE

A second NDE while on a National Geographic sponsored expedition to the Darwin Icecap in Tierra del Fuego during 1966 added to his search for meaning and truth. Caught in a blizzard and in a state of starvation, Hart lost consciousness and found another part of himself viewing the scene below as if through a telescope from another universe. He became "sure, focused, calm, and remote" from his surroundings.

The "Phaselock Code," as Hart defines it, is the field of hidden information in the fabric of reality. Phaselock refers to the idea that the information is locked together and correlated over vast distances. "Each constructs our personal reality using a small part of the information from the phaselock code," he explained his view of it. "The construction process is subconscious and most of the time we are unaware of it. It is a matter of choosing among infinite possible interpretations." As he further viewed it, during an NDE and during transcendental moments the normal construction process is abandoned, allowing the experience of an expanded reality through a part of our higher mind that connects directly to the phaselock code.

"I am not the first person to realize that the mind survives the body, or that the reality of the universe is a marvelous field of information and infinite potentials," he mused, "or that we ourselves create time by opening static time capsules in the field of information. But I had the joy of discovering these ideas independently before I was exposed to them by others."

14

An NDE on the Battlefield

~

October 24, 2016

Sometime during or around April 1969, I was sitting in an open-air theater on the roof of a three- or four-story building occupied by the USO (United Services Organizations) in central Saigon. Every few minutes, the skies about 20 miles or more away – to the southeast, I think – would light up and we'd hear bombs exploding, as the building we were sitting atop of rattled a little. It was somewhat surreal as the movie we were watching was "The Green Berets," starring John Wayne. It was about the Vietnam War, the very war that was lighting the skies and shaking our building. I recall thinking about how strange it was that I was watching a movie about a war that I could see taking place in the distance. I wondered where reality began and left off.

As I read *If Morning Never Comes: A Soldier's Near-Death Experience on the Battlefield*, recently released by White Crow Books, I wondered if Bill Vandenbush, the author, was seeing and hearing the same thing that I did that very night, because it was during April 1969 that he suffered severe combat wounds and had a near-death experience somewhere south of Saigon, the victim of friendly bombs dropped in the wrong place. Perhaps he had already been air-evacuated to a military hospital in Japan by that time or maybe it was just before his body was torn apart and he had his NDE. He may have been sloshing his way through some rice paddy on a patrol mission. My military days were well over by that time and I was in Vietnam in a civilian capacity while investigating some large insurance claims. The Viet Cong didn't seem to concern themselves with Americans in civilian clothes and in non-military vehicles with local drivers.

During his youth, Vandenbush idolized John Wayne, seeing him as the ultimate warrior, even though Wayne never spent a day in the military. "I had grown up in the John Wayne generation, learning about war from the Hollywood perspective where every man was a hero and every soldier was adored by his nation and its people," he writes. "I was greatly influenced by John Wayne's macho image and the respect he commanded. In the movies, John Wayne was always a hero."

But after Vandenbush joined the Army in 1968 he began to realize that it was not nearly as glamorous as Hollywood made it out to be. "The horror, the evil, the violence, the blood, guts, and death of war are so far removed from living and training in the U.S. that it was impossible to fully grasp the significance and long-term effect of that experience without being there," he continues, adding that it never occurred to him how horrific it would be when he saw his friends die or how traumatic it would be to shoot at a real person. Nevertheless, there was still a little Boy Scout in him and he expected, at age 18, that it was all part of becoming a man.

He recalls that on his first patrol his mouth became dry and he began to sweat profusely. When he couldn't sweat anymore, it felt like his body was on fire. "I started to shake and felt like my head was coming apart. We had only been walking about ten minutes but every step was pure torture ... I was hyperventilating and I had dry heaves; my heart was pounding loudly and I couldn't control my fear. I thought I was going to die of fright. Never in my short life had I felt so much fear."

In a matter of time, however, his fear was replaced by a sense of pride, a sense of teamwork, as he worked together with a large group of men in a coordinated effort, utilizing high tech, modern warfare equipment that gave him a feeling of invincibility. He began to feel just like John Wayne.

Life Imitating Art

It was suddenly life imitating art. It was while leading a squad on a patrol that things went wrong – that a bomb dropped by an American plane made him a victim of the war. He recalls lying in the dust and dirt of a dry rice paddy, seeing waves of heat rising from the ground, his men safe on the other side of the rice paddy, and the enemy still firing at them. He took off his helmet and saw his right eye fall into it. "Once I had accepted death and knew there was nothing I could do to avoid it, all the worry, fear, and pain faded away," he recalls. "All that was left to do was relax and let it happen. However, as he curled up on the ground he was "suddenly struck by an incredible feeling of peace and tranquility." He felt suspended from time and space, between the here-and-now and the here-ever-after. He experienced a dark tunnel but felt bathed in a soft light as he continued to glide forward. As the light washed over him, he felt an incredible sense of calm. And then he was thrust into a bright white light and he no longer possessed a body. Everything was beautiful and totally fulfilling. He felt that he was in a different dimension, one in which he encountered his grandfather, who had died several years earlier. While talking with his grandfather, a "ball of energy" appeared and told him that he must return to his earthly place and fulfill his higher purpose before again coming to the Light. There's much more to it than that, but that's the gist of it.

Vandenbush's recovery was slow and challenging, and there was much adversity to overcome in continuing on in the earthly life, including two divorces and many job frustrations. His injuries went well beyond his eye, especially affecting his throat and arm. The doctors treating him were not hopeful and even recommended amputation of the arm, but Vandenbush rejected such a procedure. "The glow from the Light and the guidance from Spirit were so intense and so complete, that I responded to the constant negative prognosis with, 'They just don't know what they're talking about. They're wrong. Everything is going to be okay.'" He writes that the negativity he constantly experienced paled in comparison to the all-encompassing peace and sense of well-being and fulfillment he experienced with the Light.

It was his experience in the Light that kept him going. "I was slowly becoming aware that my wounds were part of my destiny and part of my higher purpose in life," he muses. Whenever he encountered hard times, he called upon "Spirit" to get him through them, and he always managed to succeed in overcoming the adversity.

Vandenbush's story was originally told in a 2003 book, but he has had another NDE since then, one in which Spirit again communicated with him during the week in which he was in a coma. He states that this time he went beyond the White Light and was taken on an incredible journey through the universe, observing dimensions and layers that are far more vast than the simple material existence we experience on earth. It is a very inspiring story, especially for the person who doesn't appreciate adversity and blames all his or her misfortunes on God.

15

Retired Naval Architect Tells of His NDE

~

March 24, 2016

When Dr. Alan Ross Hugenot had a near-death experience in 1970, it didn't have a name and he was reluctant to talk about it. But he now says "the best thing that ever happened to me was when I 'died' in a motorcycle wreck."

It wasn't until 2006, as he approached retirement from his career as a naval architect and marine engineer, that he began seriously exploring consciousness, including mediumship. Now, 10 years later, Hugenot is an evidential medium, serving as a test medium for the Consciousness Research Laboratory at the Institute of Noetic Sciences, where he works with Drs. Dean Radin and Arnaud Delorme.

After growing up in North Hollywood, Calif., Hugenot served in the U.S. Navy during the Vietnam War. He then studied mechanical engineering at Oregon Institute of Technology and began his career in the design department of Puget Sound Naval Shipyard in Washington. He eventually worked at "nearly every shipyard" in the country, on all three coasts and the

Great Lakes. Along the way, he earned a Doctorate of Science in mechanical engineering.

Although "retired," Hugenot, who is married to Gale and lives in San Francisco, serves on a number of engineering standards writing committees and as chairman of the Motor Yacht and Service Craft Panel of the Small Craft Committee for the Society of Naval Architects and Marine Engineers. He is frequently asked to write and deliver papers on various aspects of naval engineering for other organizations. He also works occasionally as an expert witness in maritime cases.

I had the opportunity to interview Hugenot for the February issue of *The Searchlight*, a publication of The Academy for Spiritual and Consciousness Studies and am pleased to offer that interview here.

Alan, please summarize your NDE.

"It was during May 1970 when I was attending college after serving in the Navy. Briefly, I was severely injured in a motorcycle accident, lapsed into a coma for 12 hours, traveled out-of-body where I communed on the other side with a *Being of Light*. After returning to the body, and regaining consciousness, I remained hospitalized for 33 days.

"This was five years before Dr. Raymond Moody published his book, *Life After Life*, in which he coined the term 'near-death experience.' Back in those dark ages, the standard medical procedure was to treat all NDEs as delusions. Consequently, the resident psychiatrist, after attempting to reason with me but finding he was unable to convince me of my error, decided that if I would not conform to his version of reality he would commit me to the insane asylum. This 'punishment' was for merely making such insane claims about, 'having died and then come back to life.'"

I gather you didn't keep the experience to yourself as so many people do.

"Yes, and one of the questions the psychiatrist put to me was, 'Just where do you think such a place as the afterlife could exist?' I didn't help my case any by responding, 'Doctor, I respect all your learning and degrees, but it is like I've been to Mexico and you haven't, and I want to tell you about my experience. But, instead of listening to me, and discovering a new country, you are telling me that based on your superior knowledge and training that you're sure that Mexico is impossible and so cannot exist, and that I must therefore be mistaken. Isn't that a little closed minded?

"Luckily, my orthopedic surgeon, was not so backward in his medical technology, and so discharged me from the hospital a few days early, just ahead of the psychiatrist completing the papers to have me committed."

Why did it take you some 40 years to start talking about your NDE and writing about it and related topics?

"Early on, after the NDE, burdened with visceral personal knowledge of an inconvenient truth, and being unable to reconcile it with society's standard model of reality, I quickly learned to be quiet about what I knew. Instead, and unlike the other SET (Science, Engineering & Technology) students, I began to also study philosophy, history, logic, meta-physics in evening classes, beginning a research odyssey which has now spanned 46 years, investigating multiple scientific disciplines, collating data and verifying the science supporting what I knew.

"When an event or experience occurs, which has no explanation within the current scientific framework, it is considered an *anomaly*. By being killed and coming back I had myself become a scientific *anomaly*. But, it is such anomalies which stubbornly refuse to go away that eventually act as the catalyst for a new advance in science. Today, I am welcomed as a featured speaker."

What were your early religious or spiritual views?

"I was raised in a fundamentalist Baptist home. My own views were discounted by my parents, and so when I left for the Navy I investigated all the various religions with Navy chaplains. I later became a Lutheran (Missouri Synod) because they seemed to actually study their Bible rather than carry it around like an anchor without opening it. But, prior to the NDE, if you had asked me what I thought happened after death I would have said, 'My church believes there is a heaven and a hell, but I'm not so sure what happens.

"Today, my sister thinks that because I am an evidential medium I have gone the way of the devil. And so she refuses to talk to me. But, while receiving readings from mediums who do not know me, my mother has come through from the other side with excellent evidential information, to tell me that she is sorry for both her fundamentalism, and also for leading my sister astray."

So how have your views changed?

"The primary lesson I learned while out-of-body was that we are not physical beings, but are instead eternal spirits temporarily occupying physical bodies. The NDE moved me toward eastern meditative traditions, the Unity School or Practical Christianity and finally, as I became a medium, into Spiritualism. But I do not believe in a hell or retribution, and I do believe in universal salvation (everyone has eternal life). I came to realize that the Newtonian box I had been trained to use in my work as an engineer is only a fragment of the story of the conscious universe. In a larger sense, I also learned that our 350-year-old paradigm of classical Newtonian physics, limited to three dimensions plus time, did not include everything. In fact, it fell far short and only included a very small corner of a much larger universe. I realized materialist science was deeply flawed in its world view.

"I believe that the only scientific way to understand mediumship is to do it yourself, so I took a correspondence course in mediumship from the Morris Pratt Institute, and then later attended the course in evidential mediumship at Arthur Findlay College in England. I now know unequivocally that we continue after death in alternative dimensions of existence, but I want to better understand the precise physics and biology behind it all."

To what extent have you developed your mediumship?

"All I can do is point to the evidence. Once, while working on the platform before a Spiritualist church, I brought through five spirits in a row, related to three sitters. I gave their accurate names and relationships without guessing. When you look at the statistics just on the names, the odds are 320 billion to one of getting all of them. But, if you take into account the fact that I also gave their correct relationships to the sitters, with odds of say one in 12, (mother, father, sister, brother, uncle, aunt, cousin, grandma, grandpa, great grandma, great grandpa, friend), the odds become astronomical, roughly 79.6 quadrillion to one. So, I have to ask...how did I get that information? How can it not be spirit talking to me?"

Some parapsychologists would say you received it telepathically from the sitter or, if it is information the sitter didn't have, that you accessed it from a relative or friend of the sitter on the other side of the country.

"I can't prove that is not the case and there is no science to prove it one way or the other, but it makes much more sense to me that it is spirit talking to me rather than getting it through telepathy or remote viewing of some kind. I think Occam's Razor favors spirit communication over telepathy or remote viewing, especially when you are talking about tapping into the consciousness of someone not even present. How did I find that person and how did I extract that bit of information from his consciousness?"

What if the skeptical scientist asks you how consciousness can go on without a functioning brain?

"Same answer. I state that this can only be true for someone who believes the brain creates consciousness. How could a cold dead universe develop life? And how could that life develop consciousness? Isn't that a miracle that even Jesus could not produce? Therefore, the universe must have already been conscious. And, everything even those 'dead' stones are made of consciousness. This is what materialism can't quite believe, but it is no problem for QED and biocentrism."

I understand that you have authored a new book which will be published early this year. How will it differ from your first book?

"Everyone wants me to talk about the science of the afterlife, which was scrunched into just one chapter of my 2012 book, becoming my 2016 book, *The New Science of Consciousness Survival*, which has a foreword by Dr. Gary Schwartz, discusses how the sciences of quantum electro-dynamics, near-death experiences, biocentrism and the sciences of consciousness survival have already replaced Newtonian materialism, at least for those scientists with the intellectual honesty and scientific rigor to examine the extensive and overwhelming data and to pay attention to what it means. "When we can't discern 96 percent of what exists in our universe, there is plenty of spare room for all kinds of unknowns – much more than just the afterlife's 'undiscovered country from whose bourn no traveler returns,' but entire undiscovered galaxies, alternative dimensions, multi-verses, etc., etc. Hopefully, this book will make all this easily understandable in a simple way, showing how materialism has always been merely speculation based on several untrue presuppositions, and also how the evolving scientific world view based on quantum electro-dynamics allows the existence of psi, the para-normal and consciousness survival, to all be valid."

Do you sometimes feel like you are preaching to the choir, that no real progress is being made in getting your message across?

"No, actually I see great progress. Forty-six years ago they wanted to put me in the nut house, but now I am the featured speaker at numerous organizations. Materialism is on its last legs and the meta-paradigm is shifting."

16

A Physician Discusses
Her NDE Research

~

April 10, 2017

"It is impossible to be so close to the cutting edge of life and death and not be transformed by it in some way. Our beliefs and opinions about life and death are shaped by what we encounter." So writes Laurin Bellg, M.D., in her recent book, *Near Death in the ICU.*

Dr. Bellg, a board-certified critical care physician and Chair of Medicine and ICU director for two intensive care units in the Appleton, Wisconsin area, draws upon some 20 years of experience in attending to critically ill and dying patients. "Although it was within the hallowed halls of my conventional medical training that I first encountered patient accounts of the unusual and mysterious during near-death moments, extreme illness and trauma, it has only been within the past few years that I have begun to pay serious attention not only to the medical care of my patients but also to their personal experiences as they approach death," she offers in the book's

Introduction, adding that her own thoughts about life and death have morphed over the years, due in part to the accounts of transcendent experiences.

She begins by telling of her experience with another physician, an 87-year-old dying patient she refers to as "Dr. John." He told her that he was not afraid to die and related a near-death experience (NDE) he had during WWII, when the jeep he occupied was hit by mortar fire. Dr. John recalled floating above his body in the operating room and found it strange to be watching his friends and colleagues in such a detached manner as they fought to save him. "He felt completely weightless and peaceful, void of any fear. The feeling of love was immense, almost unbearable, and recalling it now, Dr. John's voice became fragile as he paused to fight back tears."

As Dr. Janice Holden, who has been researching NDEs since the mid-1980s, states in the afterword of the book, this is not just another "ho-hum" book about near-death experiences. "To my knowledge," she writes, "no one has addressed so well the need to offer a helpful response to those reporting an NDE, and the process of reconsidering one's belief system in light of the evidence from NDEs."

I recently had the opportunity to interview Dr. Bellg for *The Searchlight*, a publication of The Academy for Spiritual and Consciousness Studies, Inc. A slightly abridged version of that interview is presented here.

Dr. Bellg, what were your beliefs relative to life after death prior to having the various deathbed and near-death experiences you report in your book? How have they "morphed"?

"It is impossible to be exposed to death-bed and near-death experiences and not be affected by them, but what I can say with certainty is after being privileged to have heard so many accounts of near-death experiences, I'm not afraid to die. What comes next, though, I really don't know, but I believe something does. And I'm beginning to think that what it looks like to us from this vantage point is heavily influenced by our culture and belief systems. My Christian patients see a Christian construct. My Hmong and Native American patients see an ancestor-based construct. My Asian Indian patients see a heavily-Hindu-informed construct. I've come to the comfortable conclusion that something of us, like our consciousness, survives, but what that is or what it looks like I really don't know. Even experiencers have a hard time putting it into words. Because we are so very influenced by the lenses through which we are peering to behold an experience, a pure and unadulterated interpretation may elude us. I've forgotten who said, 'What we see is what we believed before we looked,' but I believe there is a lot of truth in that statement."

Is there any one patient or NDE that especially moved you? If so, would you mind summarizing it?

"I will always remember Samuel, whom I spoke of in my book. He was the first patient I'd taken care of who seemed to have had an anomalous experience. This was literally within weeks of me graduating from medical school, so I was still a very new doctor and heavily indoctrinated into a left-brain, science-based way of looking at things. I believe he died because I failed to recognize an out-of-body experience he had during surgery and as a result he refused further operations that he needed to survive. He reported seeing his whole surgery, including his open abdomen, from a vantage point above his body and was able to describe it in detail while feeling no pain. He was so freaked out by it that he refused any further life-saving interventions. I had no context with which to frame what he had experienced and help him deal with it. I had not been taught that in medical school. As I explain in my book, I still hold Samuel's memory very close as motivation to help patients sort out anomalous experiences that don't fit neatly into the scaffolding of our current understanding of the physical universe. Samuel's experience (and mine with Samuel) propelled me on a journey to support patients in their unusual experiences – whatever they may be – and to understand as much as I could about them."

What about deathbed visions or other deathbed phenomena, such as "soul mist"?

"Even physicians who downplay the near-death experience acknowledge that patients who are dying often appear to talk to relatives who have already passed away that we cannot see but they apparently can. It has become an unofficial metric to inform family members that their loved one is close to passing because they are beginning to communicate with predeceased loved ones. I'll be honest, I've not heard of 'soul mist' but imagining what you might be referring to, I recently had a whole team of caregivers, including a doctor and several nurses, speak of a very strange wind that went through the room at the time the patient officially died."

You state that discussion of these transcendent experiences by patients is not a "safe" topic with your peers. Have you seen any changes in this regard over your 20 years of practicing medicine?

"Sadly, not really. Chaplains in my healthcare system continue to report accounts that patients have spontaneously shared with them. Spiritual leaders seem to be safe space around such phenomenon. How can we facilitate a culture of presumed safe space as care givers? That is my question to my medical community. And, that is the primary reason I felt compelled to write my book. I thought that I had something important to contribute to the discussion about near-death experiences and how to be able to converse with someone about their anomalous experience of consciousness is a fundamental part of good patient care."

Have you had much feedback from your skeptical peers about your book? If so, how do they react to it?

"I have had some feedback, yes, and it has mostly been positive. Those who disagree have politely avoided engaging me in conversation about it, but fortunately it has not interfered with our professional relationship. A couple of doctors I work with have come forward telling me they actually had a near-death experience and that they confirmed it was not safe to talk about it in today's medical environment if you expect to have a respectable medical career. I have to admit I was very reluctant to write this book and once I'd done it there was a part of me that hoped no one would actually read it! Especially people I work with. But now that it is out there and I still have my job, I'm feeling a bit braver about being more open. Conventional medicine is a very powerful machine and strongly founded on evidence-based practices. I understand that and, for the most part, agree with it. As body mechanics we need to be confident that the medicines we give and the procedures we do are not only safe for our patients but that they also are going to work and produce a good outcome. That is being responsible. But there is this whole other side to what it means to be a human patient that involves experiences that we cannot measure or reliably reproduce. We need to cultivate a new way of integrating these experiences that are very real to the patient and honor them. Telling the patient it didn't happen because we, the measurers of phenomenon, didn't see it is not only unhelpful, it is very disrespectful. And, as in Samuel's case, potentially deadly. That is not good patient care."

What are your views on all the mechanistic theories relative to NDEs, such as oxygen deprivation, hallucinations, stress hormones, etc.?

"Sure, those things happen, but those experiences then become muddled, disjointed and don't take away a patients fear of death.

Patients hallucinate and oxygen deprivation can cause visual disturbance, but there is a distinct clarity around out-of-body experiences during severe trauma and near-death states that patients often recall in exquisite, organized detail. Furthermore, the nature of transformation that patients experience just doesn't happen during states of delirium, hallucinations or stress hormone surges. Again, my stance remains that we are talking about something that the experiencer can't prove did happen and the non-experiencer cannot prove did not happen, so we need to have a different approach to discussing these transformative events in a way that serves the patient we have taken an oath to care for and protect. I'm not sure that at this point in our human evolution we have the science to explain what is happening. Maybe we will never be able to. All the more reason to create a space where we can discuss the phenomenon without shaming the experiencer."

You mentioned in the book hearing a physician interviewed on the radio tell an NDEr that he was likely hallucinating. If you, as a director of an ICU, were to overhear a young physician in the ICU offering a similar explanation to a concerned patient, how would you handle it?

"I have actually heard that said in my ICU and have intervened on the patient's behalf to facilitate a different discussion without making either the patient or the health care provider feel bad. No one should feel uncomfortable or shamed around such an important topic. I am also an ICU attending, so when residents rotate through to work with me for a month at a time, we talk about it and I give them a copy of my book to read as an assignment. I really hope that how I have learned to facilitate this discussion over the past twenty years can offer these young doctors a short cut. Interestingly, a couple of nurses have pointed out that their curriculum often has a brief section to deal with such occurrences and the overriding theme in their training material is to respect it even if you don't understand or agree with it. I was so impressed when a nurse brought in a textbook from her conventional nursing training program associated with our State university system and pointed out a short section on talking with patients about their near-death experience. My vision is to see that in physician textbooks!"

The NDE has been studied now for more than 40 years. Aren't we well past the point of diminishing returns in what we can learn from them?

"Maybe, but continuing to ask the question and hold the phenomenon lighting in curious regard puts us in a better place to eventually understand it. Humans saw fire for much longer than that – millennia even – before they finally sorted out that it wasn't a god or evil spirit and that they could even make it! It took longer still to uncover all of its uses and applications. The same for electricity and other things that were once so mysterious that we now take for granted as a normal part of our daily lives. I don't know that we have the right science or even the right sort of brain to yet understand the near-death and out-of-body experience, but that doesn't mean we should stop asking the question. Another example I give in my book is that for thousands of years early civilizations thought that jars of grain slurries left out in the open air were magically turned into alcoholic beverages by spirits. It wasn't until many thousands of years later that science was able to inform us that wind currents carried yeast spores that settled into the liquid and did the magical transformation called fermentation."

17

From Surgeon to Superman

~

November 26, 2012

When Dr. Eben Alexander took the speaker's platform at the Forever Family Foundation conference in Phoenix on November 10, he looked very much like that meek, mild-mannered reporter known as Clark Kent. At the conclusion of his talk, for which he received a standing ovation, Alexander appeared to have been transformed into a Superman, of sorts.

There was no indication that Alexander, a renowned academic neurosurgeon, was faster than a speeding bullet or able to leap tall buildings in a single bound, but the audience of some 200 appeared to have seen him as more powerful than a locomotive, the locomotive in this case called Materialism or Scientism – a belief system propelling mankind toward an abyss of nothingness. It was as if a bridge high above the abyss was out and Alexander had firmly planted himself in front of the locomotive, offering enough resistance to at least slow its "progress" as it approached the bridge for its fatal plunge into the abyss.

Four years ago and some miles earlier, when the locomotive was steaming down the tracks, Alexander was one of its passengers, more or less subscribing to the philosophy of materialism. "I thought I knew how we are all put together," he explained his attitude at the time, adding that he had since come to realize that the boundaries of science need to be greatly extended. "I was on an express train out of here."

Alexander told of his personal derailment, referring to November 10, 2008, exactly four years to the day before his Phoenix talk, when he contracted a case of severe E. coli bacterial meningitis, a condition that put him in a coma for seven days. "I should have died, should not have come back," he said, mentioning that he had a disease that was virtually impossible for him to have.

It was what he experienced during his coma that converted Alexander to a belief in life after death – "a beautiful, incredible dream world," as he describes it in his recently released book, *Proof of Heaven: A Neurosurgeon's Journey into the Afterlife*, published by Simon and Schuster and now number 2 among all books at Amazon.com. "Except it wasn't a dream. Though I didn't know where I was or even what I was, I was absolutely sure of one thing: this place I'd suddenly found myself in was completely real."

I'll leave the details of Alexander's experience to his book, but will dwell here more on the reaction to his experience by those stuck in the muck and mire of scientism. (I know I overuse that metaphor, but I can think of nothing better to describe it.) One of the first to attack Alexander's conclusions regarding his near-death experience was Dr. Sam Harris, a neuroscientist and popular author, including a best-seller titled *The End of Faith*. In his blog of October 12, before Alexander's book was even released, Harris called a Newsweek magazine story about Alexander's experience as something which "is best viewed as an archaeological artifact that is certain to embarrass us in the eyes of future generations."

As of this writing, there have been 422 reviews of Alexander's book at Amazon, the majority giving it the highest rating, five stars. However, the fundamentalists of both religion and science have done their best to bring down the overall rating by giving it only one star, the lowest rating possible. The religious fundamentalists are disappointed and skeptical because Alexander didn't see Jesus, while the scientific fundamentalists scoff, commenting that there is no scientific "proof."

A White Crow

Dr. Richard Brannon, a retired biologist who heard Alexander's talk in Phoenix, was very much impressed and referred to Alexander as a "white crow," a term coined by Professor William James of Harvard during the 1880s and applied to Leonora Piper, probably the most-tested medium of all time. She was studied for some 25 years by a number of esteemed scientists, including James, Dr. Richard Hodgson, Sir Oliver Lodge, and Dr. James Hyslop, all of them initially skeptical but concluding that she was not a charlatan, and that she possessed supernormal powers of some kind. There was a belief among the uninformed of that time that all mediums were tricksters and the white crow label pinned on Mrs. Piper by James was intended to clearly indicate that a true medium existed.

Brannon was not suggesting that all other near-death experiencers are "black crows." He has studied numerous NDE accounts and believes that NDE research has provided strong evidence that we are more than a physical body – that our spirit body, soul body, etheric body, whatever name is attached to it, separates from the physical body at death and enters into another realm of existence. What Brannon was saying is that the circumstances of Alexander's NDE – the fact that his cortex was completely shut down and that his body was under close medical observation during the seven days he was in a coma – make it especially evidential. According to Alexander, who should know, there is no way he should have experienced any type of consciousness during the time he was in a coma. And yet, he experienced something so profound that there in now no doubt in his mind that we are more than our brains and bodies and that consciousness does not end in death.

To those already believing in an afterlife, Dr. Alexander's story helps them move from blind faith to true faith, or conviction. To the open-minded skeptic – the true skeptic – it gives them something to ponder while providing hope that death is not the end. Unfortunately, however, there are the closed-minded individuals who are not moved by any evidence, no matter how impressive. They call it all "unscientific," without even understanding the scope of science. They have a will to disbelieve. I believe Alfred Russel Wallace, co-originator with Charles Darwin of the natural selection theory of evolution, summed it up best when he said, "The antagonism which it excites seems to be mainly due to the fact that [a spirit world] is, and has long been in some form or other, the belief of the religious world, and of the ignorant and superstitious of all ages, while a total disbelief in spiritual existence has been the distinctive badge of modern scientific skepticism."

It has been my observations that many, if not most, of the pseudoskeptics do not take the time to distinguish between the superstitions and follies of religion and the findings of valid psychical research and parapsychology. Brannon mentions discussing the subject with another retired biologist, a confirmed materialist whose mind was made up and who had absolutely no interest in hearing about the evidence for the survival of consciousness.

In another recently-released book, *Science Set Free*, Dr. Rupert Sheldrake, a world-renowned scientist and a clear exception to the more fundamentalist scientist, points out that many scientists are unaware that materialism is an assumption. "They simply think of it as science," Sheldrake states, "or the scientific view of reality, or the scientific worldview. They are not actually taught about it, or given a chance to discuss it. They absorb it by a kind of intellectual osmosis." Sheldrake adds that "Despite all the achievement of science and technology, materialism is now facing a credibility crunch that was unimaginable in the twentieth century."

It is people like Dr. Eben Alexander who are contributing to this credibility crunch. Clearly, it takes courage to place oneself in front of a locomotive, even if that locomotive is losing steam from other forces, but truth is a strong motivator.

Part IV

Science Examines the NDE

Acceptance of the findings of near-death researchers would mark the beginning of the end of a culture whose driving forces have been greed and ambition, and which measures success in terms of material possessions, wealth, reputation, and social status. The present culture, therefore, has an enormous vested interest in undermining near-death research, which it does through ignoring, debunking, and otherwise marginalizing the research.

More subtly, our culture has created an atmosphere of 'taboo,' for want of a better name, around any serious discussions of spirituality. This is why we tend to feel uneasy and awkward in discussing these things with colleagues. To avoid these feelings of discomfort and anxiety generated by the taboo, academics try to protect themselves by employing the same strategies that everyone uses to avoid anxiety.

The first strategy is denial. By paying no attention to the research, by ignoring it and dismissing it a priori, the academic is spared the uncomfortable feelings that would arise from violating the taboo. The second strategy is to debunk, to explain away, and to otherwise marginalize the research, and sometimes even the researchers themselves.

—**Neal Grossman, Ph.D.**

18

Has the NDE Been Debunked?

~

September 3, 2012

While Near-Death Experiences (NDEs) have been reported for centuries, it was not until the 1970s when Drs. Elisabeth Kubler-Ross and Raymond Moody, both American psychiatrists, brought it into the public view with books on the subject. The implication of the NDE is that we do in fact have two bodies, as St. Paul told us – a physical one and a spiritual one. Or to put it another way, the research strongly suggests that the mind is separate from the brain and is able to operate independently of the physical body.

NDE researchers have identified six basic characteristics associated with the NDE:

1. Seeing things from outside the body as in observing one's operations from above or viewing an accident scene from outside the accident.
2. A feeling that one is in a tunnel and that he or she is proceeding through that tunnel toward a light at the end of the tunnel.

3. Being greeted by deceased relative or friends who act as a guide, by an angel, or by a Being of Light, and then receiving some kind of orientation relative to the person's situation.
4. A life review in which the person sees every instant of her or his life flash in front of her/him.
5. Being told by the Being of Light, the "angel," guide or relative that he/she must return to the body, and usually protesting it.
6. A complete transformation in the person's outlook, generally moving from a materialistic outlook to a spiritual one.

Although many of the NDE stories are impressive and convincing, the "debunkers" – those cynical scientific fundamentalists whose have made science their religion while claiming to be skeptics – have attempted to come up with arguments opposing the idea that mind and brain are separate. I've rarely, if ever, seen all the arguments advanced by skeptics and debunkers addressed at one time. However, R. Craig Hogan, Ph.D. addresses all of them in *Your Eternal Self,* a comprehensive overview of all the evidence for the argument that we are eternal beings temporarily housed in a physical shell. "… all have been demonstrated to be implausible," Hogan states, referring to the debunkers' theories on the NDE. Here are the primary theories offered by the debunkers:

The Oxygen Deprivation Theory: One of the debunker's favorite theories is that the NDE is nothing more than the hallucination of an oxygen-deprived brain. "That explanation was never given credence by anyone who knows anything about the brain's function," Hogan states, pointing out that people who undergo a NDE describe their senses as being more acutely aware than they had ever been, while the person suffering from loss of oxygen is stuporous or comatose, with very little brain function.

The Dying Brain Theory: Hogan points to research indicating that a dying brain has confusional and paranoid thinking, not the alert thinking and aware observations of the NDEr. He also mentions research by Michael Sabom, M.D. showing that the NDE occurred after the brain had already passed the dying experience.

The Medication Theory: Of course, there are numerous NDEs not involving medication or drugs. But where there is some drug or medication involved, Hogan again cites the research of Michael Sabom, a Georgia cardiologist, and Melvin Morse, a professor of pediatrics, both demonstrating that the experiences are quite different from hallucinations caused by drugs. "The reports are of sensations and consciousness that are more lucid than normal, an effect opposite to that of a brain clouded by drugs," Hogan states.

The Mental Instability Theory: Some debunkers have suggested that NDEs are a result of mental instability. Hogan cites research indicating that NDE subjects were actually significantly healthier than psychiatric inpatients and outpatients and somewhat healthier than college students. He quotes Dr. Melvin Morse as saying that NDEs are predominantly positive and an acknowledgement of reality.

The Defense Against Dying Theory: Debunkers also claim that the NDE is simply a self-defense mechanism for the person who is confronted with extinction. "But this conflicts with the feeling of the enhanced self-identity that invariably occurs in an NDE," Hogan points out, going on to mention that this theory suggests a dream-like state, whereas NDEs are marked by absolute clarity.

The Religious Expectation Theory: "If it were fulfilling the experiencer's expectations of what dying is like, we would expect that only people who believed in and expected a near-death experience would have one, not suicides who anticipate annihilation, fundamentalists who expect only to see God, or agnostics and atheists who would not believe in an NDE phenomenon at all," Hogan writes, adding that this is definitely not the case.

The Cultural Expectation Theory: Hogan cites research demonstrating that different cultures have produced remarkably similar findings, thus showing that they're not dependent on expectations in any culture.

The Hearsay Theory: Some debunkers speculate that the NDE is pieced together after a trauma from bits and pieces of information gathered from medical personnel while the experiencer floated in and out of consciousness. Here again, research has shown that experiencers have observed things outside their visual fields and what is going on in the emergency room or trauma scene.

The Temporal Lobe Seizure Theory: While temporal lobe seizures produce illusions, hallucinations, and feeling of despair, these negative experiences are clearly not consistent with positive NDEs.

Hogan mentions some interesting research by Carl Becker, Ph.D., professor of comparative thought at Kyoto University and a scholar in bioethics, death, and dying. Becker determined that NDEs are real, verifiable, objective events, as 1) experiencers have clairvoyant or precognitive knowledge they could not have known that is later verified; 2) the NDE is the same across cultures and religions; 3) the NDE is different from religious expectations and are thus not fantasies; 4) in some cases, a third party has observed visionary figures seen by the experiencers, thus indicating that they are not subjective hallucinations.

"Today, humankind, especially in the West, is intellectually precocious and spiritually retarded," Hogan opines. "The result is that those areas of our lives based in technology are advanced and those that rely on understanding the meaning of life are primitive. People are engineering moon landings during their work days and going home to family conflicts, financial stress, and fear of death that leaves their lives full of tension, fear, and unhappiness."

19

Researchers Offer More Light on the NDE

~

July 12, 2010

Over the past 35 years, near-death experience (NDE) researchers like Drs. Raymond Moody, Elisabeth Kubler-Ross, Kenneth Ring, Michael Sabom, Bruce Greyson, Melvin Morse, Barbara Rommer, Sam Parnia and others have built a very solid wheel, one that supports the idea that we have a spirit body as well as a physical body and that consciousness remains with the spirit body after physical death. Close-minded skeptics keep trying to make the wheel collapse by bending the spokes and throwing obstacles in the path of the rolling wheel.

Every now and then, as happened a month or two ago, the theory that the NDE is nothing more than abnormal brain activity resulting from oxygen deficiency gets resurrected and makes its way around the Internet and the print media as if it is news rather than something that goes back 25 or more years. The pseudoskeptics' blogs make it out to be some sort of victory in their war on superstition and ignorance, and they seemingly take great pride in their 'intellectualism.'

Fortunately, new researchers come on the scene to debunk the pseudoskeptics and keep the wheel rolling. In his recently released book, *Consciousness Beyond Life*, Dr. Pim van Lommel, a world-renowned cardiologist practicing in The Netherlands, dismisses the oxygen-deprivation theory based on the fact that it is 'accompanied by an enhanced and lucid consciousness with memories and because it can also be experienced under circumstances such as an imminent traffic accident or a depression, neither of which involves oxygen deficiency.'

Van Lommel further dismisses the theory that the tunnel effect experienced by many NDErs results from a disruption of oxygen to the eye or the cerebral cortex. He points out that oxygen deficiency in these areas cannot explain meeting deceased relatives in the tunnel, as has often been reported, or hearing beautiful music. He explains why carbon dioxide overload, various chemicals, and other physiological theories do not account for the NDE. 'When new ideas do not fit the generally accepted (materialist) paradigm, many scientists perceive them as a threat,' van Lommel writes. 'It is hardly surprising therefore that when empirical studies reveal new phenomena or facts that are inconsistent with the prevailing scientific paradigm, they are usually denied, suppressed, or even ridiculed.'

Having grown up in an academic environment, van Lommel was of a materialist/reductionist mindset before he began studying the NDE and the nature of consciousness. He has closely examined all the arguments made by the scientific fundamentalists and now has a more positive outlook. 'That death is the end used to be my own belief,' he states with conviction. 'But after many years of critical research into the stories of the NDErs, and after a careful exploration of current knowledge about brain function, consciousness, and some basic principles of quantum physics, my views have undergone a complete transformation. As a doctor and researcher, I found the most significant finding to be the conclusion of one NDEr: 'Dead turned out to be not dead.' I now see the continuity of our consciousness after the death of our physical body as a very real possibility.'

In another 2010 book, *Evidence of the Afterlife*, Dr. Jeffrey Long, a radiation oncologist in Houma, Louisiana, comes to the same conclusions as van Lommel. 'Near-death experiencers almost never have confused memories that are typical of the experience of hypoxia,' he writes, (hypoxia being reduced oxygen levels in the blood and tissues). 'The fact that highly lucid and organized near-death experiences occur at a time of severe hypoxia is further evidence of the extraordinary and inexplicable state of consciousness that typically occurs during NDEs.'

No Beating Around the Bush

Many researchers, fearing professional sanctions and obloquy from their peers, beat around the bush when it comes to the life after death implications of the NDE, but, like van Lommel, Long does not cower in this respect. 'By scientifically studying the more than 1,300 cases shared with [the Near-Death Experience Research Foundation],' he writes, 'I believe that the nine lines of evidence presented in this book all converge on one central point: *There is life after death.*'

One of the more convincing aspects of the NDE for Long is the ability of some blind people to 'see' during the NDE. '... blind people who have near-death experiences may immediately have full and clear vision,' he offers. 'This is further evidence that vision in NDEs, including near-death experiences in those who are not blind, is unlike ordinary, physical vision.'

Long reports many interesting NDEs, including one by a man named Roger who was in a head-on auto accident and immediately left his body. He told of seeing events from above. 'I went into a dark place with nothing around me, but I wasn't scared. It was really peaceful there. I then began to see my whole life unfolding before me like a film projected on a screen, from babyhood to adult life. It was so real! I was looking at myself, but better than a 3-D movie as I was also capable to sensing the feelings of the persons I had interacted with through the years. I could feel the good and bad emotions I made them go through...'

Skeptics seem to have a theory for every aspect of the NDE, including the life review which so many others have reported. The skeptical take on the life review is that it is a psychological defense mechanism permitting a retreat into pleasant memories. But Long points out that many memories are not pleasant and that such unpleasant memories would not be expected in a psychological escape.

But how can a person see every moment of his life flash before him in an instant? As van Lommel sees it, many aspects of the NDE correspond with or are analogous to some of the basic principles from quantum theory, which is non-local, i.e., timeless and placeless interconnectedness. 'The findings of NDE research suggest the possibility that (nonlocal) consciousness is present at all time and will therefore last forever,' van Lommel explains. 'The content of a near-death experience suggests a continuity of consciousness that can be experienced independently of the body.'

Lost Dentures

One of the more veridical and interesting NDEs reported by van Lommel involved a 44-year-old man brought into the hospital while in a deep coma. When a nurse started to intubate the patient, she discovered he had dentures. She removed the upper dentures and put them on a nearby cart. The patient remained comatose throughout the procedure and for a week after.

After regaining consciousness, he was returned to the coronary unit and as soon as he spotted the nurse, he asked about his dentures. '...you took my dentures out of my mouth and put them on that cart,' he told her. 'It had all these bottles on it, and there was a sliding drawer underneath, and you put my teeth there.' The patient said that he watched from above as the doctors and nurses worked on him and that he unsuccessfully tried to let them all know that he was still alive, and that they should not stop. Possibly, he was not 'unsuccessful,' since they did continue to work on him and he did survive.

Interestingly, Long reports that it takes as long as seven years or more for a person to fully integrate the NDE into his or her life. This is consistent with the biological rule that we turn over every cell in the body every seven years. It is also consistent with the 'seven-year itch' idea, which holds that there is an inclination to become unfaithful after seven years of marriage. That idea has been broadened to suggest that there is an urge to move on from any situation after seven years, whether it is a hobby or some other passion.

Organ Transplants

Something I have found particularly troubling over the years is the possibility that organs are being harvested before bodies are actually 'dead,' even though the person might be pronounced 'clinically dead.' Van Lommel devotes several interesting pages to the debate on this subject, pointing out that when brain death has been diagnosed, 96 percent of the body is still alive. While not in principle opposed to organ transplants, van Lommel suggests that more consideration should be given to the nonphysical aspects of organ donation, including the fear of death. As I interpret his comments, he is saying that perhaps that in many organ failure situations we should let nature take its course and not concern ourselves so much with surviving in this world.

Long quotes Sir John Eccles, a Nobel Prize-winning neuroscientist who studied consciousness: "I maintain that the human mystery is incredibly demeaned by scientific reductionism, with its claim in promissory materialism to account eventually for all of the spiritual world in terms of patterns of neuronal activity. This belief must be classed as superstition...We have to recognize that we are spiritual beings with souls existing in a spiritual world as well as material beings with bodies and brains existing in a material world."

20

Finding The Truth in The Light

~

March 5, 2012

Ever since reading Dr. Raymond Moody's seminal book on near-death experiences in 1975, I have read at least 50 books dealing with the near-death experience (NDE). If I were to rank them by what I call the "4 INs" – Interesting, Informative, Intriguing, and Inspirational – I'm reasonably sure that one that has been on the New York Times best seller list for 53 weeks (not consecutive) would be at the very bottom of the list, having sold more than six-million copies. I struggled to read it and tossed it aside several times before finally finishing it, just to see if the best of it might be in the closing pages.

The book was written by a Christian minister and the boy saw Jesus during his NDE. Thus, it appeals to the Christians of the world, especially the evangelicals and fundamentalists. What I don't get is how all the evangelicals and fundamentalists can be so enamored of this little boy's NDE and so repulsed by nearly all other NDEs.

Is the NDE real only if the person sees Jesus and the experience is otherwise consistent with scripture? Or, could it be that that all other NDEs are real but demonic in nature? Of course, the closed-minded skeptic would say they are all hallucinations of an oxygen-deprived brain.

There would be four or five books in contention for number one on my list, but I doubt that any of them sold even a small fraction of six million copies. One of the contenders for top spot would be *The Truth in the Light* by Dr. Peter Fenwick and Elizabeth Fenwick. This book was first published in 1995 and recently republished by White Crow Books. It offers dozens of NDE's as intriguing, if not more so, than the best seller, and some of them involve the experiencer seeing Jesus.

"Then I was pulled up through the roof and I had this glorious sense of freedom," the Fenwicks quote one experiencer, who had been blind since she was three months old and had an NDE at age 22 during a three-day coma after being in an auto accident. "I could move wherever I wanted to. I was above the street, above the hospital, and I was ecstatic about being able to move wherever I wanted to. Then that ended suddenly. I was sucked into a tunnel, and heard a sound like monstrous fans. It was not actually that, but it's the closest way I can describe it. It was a beautiful sound. The tunnel was dark, with regular open spaces in the side, through which I could see other people traveling in other tunnels. There was one area I passed by where there was a group of drab, dull, unhappy people who were unable to move. Then I saw the distant light, and heard these hymns. The light got brighter, and I saw Him. I saw Christ. He was incredibly beautiful...There was light in and around his head, and coming out of his head like a star."

Another NDEr, a Mrs. Holyoake, told of encountering Christ and feeling the warmth of his body. "All of a sudden my eyes were drawn to the corner of the bedroom door," she related. "A brilliant light appeared – it was taking over my bedroom and as it did so I floated above my body. This place was amass with beautiful flowers – the perfumes from them was very strong – and then Jesus came walking up to me with arms outstretched. He was dressed in a long white robe, his hair to his shoulders, ginger-auburn, and he had a short beard. The nearer he got to me I could feel the warmth from his body and as his hands almost touched my face he said, 'Come!'" However, Mrs. Holyoake struggled to tell Jesus that she couldn't leave until she kissed her husband and three children goodbye. "Jesus heard me and understood, he smiled and started to walk backwards, taking his magnificent garden with him and the light."

Being of Light

According to Dr. Fenwick, a renowned British neuropsychiatrist, about a quarter of the people who reported on their experiences were aware of some spiritual presence. "Although the 'being of light' always has spiritual significance, it is only seldom that people describe seeing a particular religious figure such as Christ," he offers. "Even those people whose Christian faith is strong don't always see Christ. Much more often there is a feeling of 'coming before one's maker': the being is felt as 'God' in a very broad sense. Perhaps 'neutrally spiritual' is the nearest one can get to the feelings the being evokes." He adds that most people, whether Christians or not, have an "identikit" image of Christ, and it is very similar to the one described by Mrs. Holyoake. "I think we have to make a distinction between the feeling of the presence of Christ in the experience, and the image which the perceiving brain creates to fit it, which is simply drawn from the picture-bank of memory."

Fenwick also found that accounts of childhood NDEs were much more likely than those of adults "to include descriptions of a very concrete Heaven, peopled by angels, Jesus figures and golden gates." He points out that the younger the child, the odder it is that he or she should have any conceptual awareness of death. "The ability to think in abstract terms (and one's own death is a fairly abstract concept) does not usually develop until later in childhood," he continues. "And yet, without the conceptual awareness, why should they have the experience at all – unless it has some sort of independent reality?"

So how are we to interpret all of this? On the one hand, we become very suspicious – and the pseudoskeptics laugh – at the idea of Jesus or another "being of light" who wears clothes and looks like we think he or she should. On the other hand, if Jesus appeared looking like Jim Caviezel, one of the movie actors who have portrayed him – short hair, no beard, and wearing modern clothes – we would suspect an impostor and the skeptics would laugh even harder. If he appeared as a ball of light, we wouldn't recognize him and the evangelicals, at least, would call it a demonic entity. The pseudoskeptics would roar with laughter.

A number of spirit messages have indicated that deceased loved ones appear to us in a way that we will recognize them, not as they have become or are in the spirit world. A spirit entity who died as a child 20 years earlier might appear to his mother in a near-death experience or upon her arrival in the spirit world as the child she knew, just for recognition purposes. It is a matter of the spirit entity projecting a thought image onto the brain of the human or the newly transitioned spirit person. It's all very mind boggling, especially when non-local time is factored into the equation.

Another very intriguing case offered by the Fenwicks involved a woman named Florence Nilsson, who claimed to have had an out-of-body experience just after she was born and was wasn't breathing. "I know it may sound absurd that a newborn infant could remember an event when so young," she testified, "but I know to this day that what I experienced actually did happen to me."

As long as mainstream science assumes that celestial matters must meet terrestrial standards, the spirit world will never be accepted, and as long as evangelicals interpret the Bible literally the NDE will remain a mystery. "We set out to test the NDE for 'reality' in a scientific way," Fenwick wraps up the book. "But I think we have to conclude that we haven't managed to explain everything. There are aspects of the experience which simply don't fit into our scientific paradigm and which seem inconsistent with a physical or even a psychological phenomenon. There remains the possibility…that the NDE is a mystical experience, and that it originates in a transcendental reality."

21

Dr. Peter Fenwick Discusses
Dying, Death and Survival

~

May 27, 2012

A neuropsychiatrist and Fellow of the Royal College of Psychiatrists, Dr. Peter Fenwick is one of the world's leading authorities on near-death experiences (NDEs). In his 1995 book, *The Truth in the Light*, co-authored with his wife, Elizabeth Fenwick, and recently republished by White Crow Books, Dr. Fenwick states that he was fascinated by the NDEs reported by Dr. Raymond Moody in his seminal book on the subject, but wondered if the "California factor" might be operating, referring to the fact that some experiments and experiences do not seem to cross the Atlantic. "My initial feeling was that near-death experiences might be only another one of these," Fenwick explained in the first chapter of his book. However, now, with some four decades of research of NDEs and the dying process behind him, Fenwick has a much better handle on the subject matter.

In addition to *The Truth in the Light,* the Fenwicks have authored *Past Lives: An Investigation into Reincarnation*

Memories (1999), *The Hidden Door: Understanding and Controlling Dreams* (1999), and *The Art of Dying* (2008). I recently interviewed Dr. Fenwick for "The Searchlight," a quarterly publication of the Academy of Spirituality and Paranormal Studies. Here is that interview:

Dr. Fenwick, what prompted your interest in this whole area of dying, death, and survival?

"My interest in death and dying and the possibility of survival was triggered by my interest in near death experiences. There is a class of NDEs which raises profound questions for neuroscience and for philosophy. It has been demonstrated in numerous studies that NDEs are reported by about 10 percent of patients who have a cardiac arrest. Dr. [Sam] Parnia and I carried out one of these studies and were able to conclude that the NDEs reported by those with cardiac arrests were no different from those reported by patients with life-threatening illness or fear of death in life-threatening situations. The question that neuroscience asks is, "can we be certain that these experiences did occur actually during the time of the cardiac arrest?" If they did, then as the features of cardiac arrest are those of the onset of the death process, it would mean that these NDEs could be a good model for the beginning of the death process.

"Thirty percent of NDEs reported during a cardiac arrest have an out-of- body experience in which the experiencer reported leaving his body and witnessing the cardiac arrest resuscitation procedure. If this is indeed true, it would mean that the NDE is taking place while the patient is unconscious and has the clinical signs of death. Michael Sabom, a cardiologist in the USA, has written widely on this issue and has compared retrospectively the accounts given by the NDEr of his experiences during cardiac arrest with those recorded in the medical notes. His data suggest that those who reported seeing the resuscitation process were accurate in what they say they observed.

"Penny Sartori, an investigator in Wales, has carried out a study on NDEs in cardiac arrest and asked those who had such an experience to describe what they saw. She also asked patients who did NOT have an NDE during their cardiac arrest to describe what they thought had happened during the resuscitation. She was able to support Sabom's observation that those who said they saw the resuscitation procedure were much more accurate than those who were asked to describe what they thought had happened.

"One of the still unanswered questions is, "exactly when do these experiences occur?" If they really do take place when the person is unconscious, then they should have no subsequent memory of them.

"Some studies are now being carried out in which cards are being put on the ceiling of rooms in coronary care units, where cardiac arrests are likely to occur, to see if these can be accurately described by people who have had an apparently veridical out of body experience. If they can, then this would time the experience, to the period of unconsciousness.

"As the evidence that we had suggested – that the NDE which was experienced during cardiac arrest was similar to that of people who were close to death – it seemed reasonable to postulate that the NDE was part of the dying process. This then triggered my interest in the dying process itself and led to the study that we carried out in hospices and a nursing home in the south of England and hospices in Rotterdam, Holland."

In "The Art of Dying," you state that the evidence points to the fact that we are more than brain function, and that consciousness will continue in some form or other after death. What do you see as the best evidence?

"The evidence for a continuation of consciousness after death is always likely to be difficult to find. The phenomena of the dying process suggest that the changes in consciousness lead to experiences for which current neuroscience has no explanation.

This suggests that it would be unreasonable to confine consciousness just to the brain and that we would expect there to be some evidence of a continuation of consciousness after death. There is some evidence for this in the phenomenon of deathbed visions. The dying often report that they are 'visited' by dead relatives shortly before they die. They tell them they have come to help them when they die and take them on a journey to elsewhere. One obvious explanation for this is that it is a 'comfort' strategy. However, we have a number of accounts of people who, as they are dying, have had a deathbed vision of a close relative who had recently died, although they did not know this. This raises the question – how did they know – and could the dead relative still exist in some form?"

Is there any one case you have studied that stands out as the most impressive or convincing? If so, would you mind summarizing that case?

"My main interest is not in the possibility of consciousness continuing in some form after death, but the changes in consciousness that occur as we die. Premonitions of death are the first and early stage. The Dalai Lama says many of us will know two years before we die that we are going to die. Although I do have accounts of people who know a number of weeks before they die that their death is imminent, this is a small group. Much more common are the phenomena which occur in the next stage of the dying process – the deathbed visions I have already mentioned. These deathbed visitors may first be seen by the dying outside the room, looking in, then, as the dying become weaker and nearer to death the visions come closer until finally they are sitting on the bed. An analysis of 100 visions showed that parents were the most common visitors, spiritual but unknown figures next, and then siblings. Angels in our sample were rarely seen as were friends.

"As the dying become weaker they may say that they are moving from one reality to another. This new reality is very much like that experienced by people who have had a near-death experience, full of love, light and spiritual beings. They may also see dead relatives who again say they will be there to help them through the dying process. The dying persons will then find themselves back in their bed again. Many are surprised at this shift of venue. The similarity of this experience to that of the NDE confirmed my feeling that the NDE in cardiac arrest can be seen as the beginning of the dying process.

"Next, some people may experience what is known as lightening up before death, or terminal lucidity, in which someone who has been unconscious, perhaps for a long period of time, suddenly wakes, sits up in bed, may greet a deathbed visitor and say they are ready to go with them, and then sink back onto the pillows and die. This is now being recognized more and more as an important time for the dying, as this brief moment of consciousness can help resolve difficulties in the family relationships.

"One of the most interesting phenomena, and perhaps the one that most defies rational explanation, occurs at the moment of death, when the dying person is reported to 'visit' someone who is emotionally close to them. Our data indicate that the visit is initiated by the dying person, and often the person visited does not know that their friend is dying, or even ill. The form the visit takes will depend on the mental state of the recipient. If they are awake, they may simply feel an awareness, perhaps of the other person's presence, or they may simply have an inexplicable sense of unease. If they are asleep the experience is in the form of a narrative dream, and is much more explicit and visual. The message given is usually that their friend is 'all right' and has come to say goodbye. (Peak in Darien)

"Finally at the time of death, shapes are seen leaving the body, radiant light may be seen in the room emanating from the body, clocks stop, and pets may become upset and behave strangely. All the phenomena which occur around the time of death or at the moment of death, suggest that consciousness may exist beyond the brain, and that communication between two people who are emotionally close but far apart is a possibility."

Why do you think mainstream science is so reluctant to recognize this evidence?

"Mainstream science has shown little interest in the mental states of the dying, and so many of these phenomena are poorly recorded and studied. The features of the experiences of the dying are not taught in medical schools so doctors know little about them. Consequently, nurses and careworkers are reluctant to talk about what they see and experience as these things are not within their culture and not accepted."

It doesn't seem like mainstream science is any closer to accepting the evidence now than it was a hundred years ago. Do you agree? Do you think there will ever be a day when mainstream science will embrace the evidence for survival?

"I do think mainstream science is beginning to take more interest in what happens when we die. Further scientific studies are likely to show that the phenomena which we have discussed above are not uncommon and can be extremely helpful both to the dying and to their bereaved families. However, if mainstream science is to accept the possibility of the survival of consciousness after death we will need a very different model of the universe. It will be one in which consciousness is central and not just an epiphenomenon. This will mean that much of science will have to be rewritten and so the acceptance of such a model is likely to take some time."

With hundreds, if not thousands, of credible near-death experiences having been recorded, what else can be achieved by NDE research? Isn't it well past the point of diminishing returns? Isn't future research now prejudiced by the fact that so many people have read or heard about NDEs?

"In 1987, I was involved in a QED TV film, *Glimpses of Death*, which was the first TV program to describe the near death experience in this country, I received over 2000 letters from people who had had such an experience. I sent out a questionnaire to 500 of these and used the questionnaire data for a book on NDEs (*The Truth in the Light*, now an e-book). What we found was that over 98 percent of people who wrote to us had not heard of NDEs when they had their own experience. A comparison of the phenomenology in this series with more recent studies of Western populations shows very little difference between them. Thus, there is little evidence from the current data that the NDE has been influenced in any way by its popularity and discussion in the media. Further cross cultural studies of the NDE would be extremely helpful, and studies to validate the veridical OBE of the NDE, particularly during a cardiac arrest, would help to show that consciousness, in certain circumstances, may exist beyond the brain and thus raise fundamental questions about the nature of consciousness itself."

Many people say that we should focus on the here-and-now, and not concern ourselves with death and after death. What is your response to them?

"I certainly agree with people who say we should concentrate on the here and now, particularly the here and now while people are dying. As I have described above, the dying have many experiences which are helpful both to them and to their families. However, we do still need more studies as the data is far from complete."

Have you come across any interesting cases since the publication of your books?

"Recently I have been able to compare the dying experiences of people who have been brought up in a rural setting with those who have been brought up in an urban environment. Although this data is preliminary it does suggest that animals appear much more prominently in the experiences of the rural group. We have accounts of birds who come into the room of the dying, are seen on their window sills and collect in large groups around the hospice at the time the person is dying. In the cases we've heard, the dying person who has had such visits has always been interested in birds and the type of birds which appear around their time of death is the one in which they have been interested. We have also had animal stories suggesting that an emotional interest and connection with animals leads to their appearance at the time of death."

Do you have any future research or book plans?

"My next project is to look into the stories of radiant light at the time of death by the use of very sensitive photometers which can measure individual photons of light. I hope to be able to chart the death process and monitor any changes in light which occur in the room of the dying. In some of our accounts of light surrounding the dying person, this light is seen by only one or two people present. This would suggest that the light is more psychological or spiritual than physical. But other accounts suggest the light is physical as it is seen reflecting off surfaces in the same way that physical light behaves. Gathering further information about why clocks stop or shapes are seen leaving the body will help us understand the importance of consciousness at the time of death and our universal interconnectedness."

22

Dr. Bruce Greyson Updates
His NDE Research

~

May 10, 2021

When I interviewed Dr. Bruce Greyson in 2004, I asked him how his research in the field of near-death experiences had influenced his beliefs concerning the survival of consciousness at death. I was not expecting him to say that the NDE proves survival, but I anticipated him saying something like "the NDE *suggests* that consciousness continues after death," or words to that effect. However, Greyson seemed to be offended by the question and replied that his belief had nothing to do with his work as a scientist or as a physician.

In an attempt to clarify my question, I asked him, in effect, if a scientist must forever sit on the fence and never have an opinion or belief. I further asked why so many scientists can commit themselves to a belief in biological evolution but not to survival. While the evidence for evolution may be very strong, I remarked, it does not appear to extend to "absolute certainty." Moreover, one does not have to be a "creationist" to be a skeptic with regard to the generally accepted belief in evolution. I was curious as to the degree of certainty a scientist must have before moving off the fence. Is his reputation as an objective researcher forever tainted if he deviates even slightly away from the mainstream worldview? If the evidence increasingly points to survival, doesn't someone have to take the lead by coming off the fence?

"...Scientists explore the evidence for and against competing hypotheses, and derive tentative conclusions that a certain hypothesis is more or less likely than others, based on the data currently available," Greyson responded to my concern. "Because science is based on empirical observation rather than revelation, our conclusions are always subject to change as new evidence accumulates. Sometimes a concept like evolution receives such overwhelming empirical support that we act as if it were proven; but even those concepts are subject to revision as we discover contradictory evidence. Although I think there is sufficient empirical evidence to make survival the most likely explanation for some phenomena, it has not been embraced by many mainstream scientists because we have much more work to do in eliminating, competing hypotheses and developing a plausible mechanism by something could survive bodily death."

At the time of the 2004 interview, I visualized Greyson sitting on a fence that separates the survival school from the nihilism school, more or less straddling it with one foot planted firmly on the nihilist's side of the fence and the other foot dangling on the survival side. Although it wasn't discussed in detail in that interview, I inferred from his answers, perhaps more from what he had to say in other writings, that he was more interested in the transformative aspects of the NDE – that is, how it helped people better enjoy their earthly lives. But that left me wondering what it was that gave rise to the positive transformations of so many NDErs if not the recognition that this life is part of a larger life and the purpose that gave it. To put it another way, if the survival aspect is not at the root of it, what causes the transformation? Were those experiencers who were transformed supposed to be happier and more fulfilled without pausing to think why? Were they mere robots? If it was because they now saw a purpose in life, was it a purpose with a humanistic/nihilistic outlook? If so, how did that view develop?

Continued Consciousness

After reading Greyson's recently released book, *After*, I now visualize him with one foot on the survival side of the fence and the other foot dangling on the nihilist's side. "I don't know whether some kind of continued consciousness after death is the best explanation for NDEs in which experiencers see deceased loved ones no one knew had died," he writes in a concluding chapter. "But I don't have any alternative explanation for the evidence. We may eventually come up with another explanation, but until then, some form of continued consciousness after death seems to be the most plausible working model."

Greyson is professor emeritus of psychiatry and neurobehavioral sciences at the University of Virginia School of Medicine. He was a co-founder of the International Association of Near-Death Studies (IANDS) and editor of the *Journal of Near-Death Studies*. He received his undergraduate degree from Cornell University in 1968 and his medical degree from the State University of New York in 1973.

During the early years of his research, Greyson struggled with the fact that NDEs "smacked of religion and folklore," which was not consistent with his upbringing in a scientific household and without any religious indoctrination. Early in his career, while on the staff of the University of Michigan, Greyson was told by the chairman of his department that he should stop wasting his time studying NDEs because they were just "anecdotes." As Greyson points out, however, personal anecdotes have been the source of most scientific hypotheses throughout history. "Most research starts with scientists collecting, verifying and comparing anecdotes until patterns in these stories become apparent, and then from those patterns emerge hypotheses, which can be tested and refined," he explains in the book.

He further explains that he is not taking sides with his materialistic friends or his spiritual friends. As he sees it, both views are plausible. "But neither of these ideas, while plausible, is a scientific premise – because there is no evidence that could ever disprove either of them. They are instead articles of belief." Whatever their source, he is convinced that NDEs "are quite real and quite profound in their impact, and are in fact important sources of spiritual growth and insight."

Greyson mentions a number of paradoxes emerging from his studies. For one, there is the extra-ordinary thinking and perceptive abilities in NDE while the brain is impaired. You'd expect just the opposite. One such ability is the life review, something experienced by a quarter of all those who participated in his 45 years of NDE research. The majority of those described the life review as more vivid than ordinary memories. Some reported that they reexperienced past events as if they were still happening.

Although many NDErs have been thought to be suffering from some kind of mental disorder, the evidence suggests, according to Greyson, that NDEs are not associated with mental disorders. He points out that people with mental disorders may lose their sense of meaning in life, feel more fearful, and become more absorbed in their own needs and concerns, but NDEs usually leads to an enhanced sense of meaning and a greater sense of connectedness with others.

The skeptics often point to studies suggesting that stimulation of certain parts of the brain can result in the sensation of leaving the body, as can seizures and certain psychedelic drugs. "Despite the common belief among some scientists that unusual electrical activity in the temporal lobe, like that caused by epileptic seizures or stimulation, can provoke experiences like NDEs or out-of-body experiences, we didn't find that to be true," Greyson states, referring to his research at an epilepsy clinic.

Oxygen Levels

The skeptics also claim that decreased oxygen in the brain is the cause of "hallucinations" reported by NDErs. However, Greyson's research, which involved measuring oxygen levels in the people during medical crises, showed that NDEs "are associated with *increased* oxygen levels, or with levels the same as those of non-experiencers. No study has ever shown *decreased* levels of oxygen during NDEs." He further mentions that patients given medication report fewer NDEs than do patients who don't get any medication.

Are people who report meeting deceased loved one during NDEs simply hallucinating? Greyson says he no longer jumps to that conclusion, although there is no way to rule out the influence of the experiencers' hopes and expectations of meeting loved ones. However, some experiencers have reported meetings with people not known to have died, which conflicts with the expectations of a reunion theory. He tells of one case in which an experiencer reported seeing his 19-year-old sister, who told him he had to go back. The experiencer was unaware that his sister had been killed in an auto accident earlier that day.

One might infer from Greyson's comments that the NDE is the only phenomenon offering evidence that consciousness survives death. As the renowned physicist Sir Oliver Lodge said, it is the cumulative evidence that convinced him. The NDE research provides icing (I prefer chocolate frosting) on the cake – a cake well baked by Lodge, Frederic Myers, Richard Hodgson, and James Hyslop long before Dr. Raymond Moody gave a name to the NDE and before Dr. Greyson was born. If one is to fully appreciate the cake, he or she needs to do more than savor the frosting. I was left wondering if Greyson is even aware of the research carried out by the pioneers of psychical research and, if he is, why he doesn't see the cumulative evidence offering the same "overwhelming" evidence that is accepted by most scientists with biological evolution. Nevertheless, having read at least 50 books on NDEs over the last 45 or so years, I would rank this book at or very near the top of the list.

Epilogue

10 Lessons Not Offered in
Sunday School or Science 101

~~~

July 26, 2020

As stated in the third article of this anthology, I have found overwhelming evidence for consciousness surviving death by the end of the nineteenth century, well before the near-death experience was identified by Dr. Raymond Moody in his 1975 book. That evidence included some near-death experiences, such as reported in Part II of this book, but the bulk of the evidence came from the investigation of mediumship by some very esteemed scientists and scholars. It is difficult to single out any single case as providing that overwhelming evidence. As Sir Oliver Lodge, a renowned British physicist and pioneer of psychical research said, it was the cumulative evidence that convinced him that consciousness continues long after death. My argument for that overwhelming evidence during the nineteenth century was set forth in my award-winning essay for the Bigelow essay contest of 2021, which can be found on line by simply putting "Bigelow essay contest winners" into a search. However, as I state in that essay, the research into other phenomena, especially the NDE, has provided "icing on the cake." Those who are not well versed in the psychical research of the twentieth century can savor the icing without the cake.

The cake with all of its icing has given us 10 lessons, as summarized in my blog of July 6, 2020, as follows:

1. Faith vs. Conviction: There is compelling evidence that consciousness survives death.
All I ever got in my catechism lessons relative to evidence are the Bible and miracles performed by a number of church saints that defied natural law. While some of those miracles really impressed me and provided a foundation for a belief in paranormal phenomena, belief was still more a matter of faith than it was conviction based on evidence. My science classes ignored the subject matter and left the student with a nihilistic worldview, but psychical research and related afterlife studies provided some solid evidence and filled in the blanks left by orthodox religion and mainstream science while also providing some explanations for the miracles taught by the Church.

2. The God Factor: Proof of God is not necessary to accept evidence that consciousness survives death.
Everything I was taught in religion classes began with the *a priori* necessity to accept the existence of an anthropomorphic God, and everything I heard from the atheistic side began with debunking the existence of that same God. The survival of consciousness, or afterlife, issue was always secondary and contingent upon proof of God. Not until I began studying psychical research did I realize that it is not necessary to have proof of God before examining and accepting the evidence for survival. One can accept survival and infer some kind of Creator or Higher Intelligence without believing in a humanlike God or subscribing to the whole "worship" side of religions. To put it another way, the evidence for survival leads to God, not the other way around.

3. No Humdrum Heaven: The Afterlife is much more dynamic than that taught by religions.

Religions teach a Heaven in which we don't do much more than praise God 24-7 while strumming harps and floating around on clouds or suffering torment in a pit of fire and brimstone. The Catholic Church teaches a middle ground in Purgatory, but it is just as bad as Hell, though not eternal. Psychical research tells us that there are many planes, spheres, dimensions, levels of vibration, whatever name be given to them, and that they are much more dynamic than the afterlife offered by religions. As Jesus said, there are "many mansions" in his Father's house. At the most populous level, the spirit world is much like our earth world, or, perhaps more accurately, the earth world is a replica of the spirit world to some extent. It is a thought world, but it is much more real than the physical world.

4. Spirit Body: We have a spiritual body, the outer rim of which is called the aura.

Different names are given to it – etheric body, astral body, celestial body, odic body, radiant body, ghost, double, phantom, subtle body, perispirit – and this body is joined to the physical body by a "silver cord," an astral umbilical cord, and threads, which are severed at death. The so-called aura, the outer edge of this spirit body, is an "electrical" field that connects us with the larger life. At the time of death, the silver cord is severed after the threads slowly break and the body emits a vaporish or misty substance, sometimes called soul mist, that forms a spirit body above the physical body. The personality continues to exist in that body at a different vibration in a different dimension of reality.

5. Hades: There is an adjustment period immediately after death.

There is a transition stage immediately following physical death in which we shed earthly habits and adapt to the spiritual environment before experiencing what has been called the "second death." This is a staging area of sorts where the soul must adjust its vibrations to the spirit world. There may be great confusion in Hades, a "fire of the mind," so to speak, by materialistic or spiritually-challenged souls; hence the belief by some religions that Hades is another name for Hell. It is said that even Jesus needed a period of adjustment. Thus, he spent a day or more in Hades and then on the third day "rose into Heaven." That is, he apparently experienced the "second death" on the "third day."

6. Awakening: We awaken on the Other Side with the degree of consciousness at which we left the material world.
Many religions would have us believe that we become all-knowing angels of some kind upon entering the spirit world, but indications are that we awaken on the Other Side with the same consciousness we had as we departed the material life. Enlightened souls awaken quickly, while more average souls awaken in something of a stupor for a period time and more depraved souls are "earthbound," not even realizing they are dead, as if in a dream world. The "awakening" depends on the degree of spiritual consciousness achieved during the earth life. While time takes on a different meaning there, it may take just a few days in earth time for the developed soul but hundreds of years in earth time for the undeveloped soul to fully awaken.

7. Judgment: There is no Judgment Day, *per se*. We judge ourselves.
In my catechism classes, I was taught that I could lead a virtuous life, but then make one big mistake, i.e., sin, before death and that would result in spending eternity in Hell. On the other hand, I could lead a life of sin, then repent on my deathbed and eventually make it to Heaven after spending a few-hundred years in Purgatory. However, psychical research and afterlife studies suggest that we judge ourselves and settle in at a level based on what has been called a "moral specific gravity" – which is a melding of all our positive and negative moral acts during our

lifetime. We can't cheat in judging ourselves because we cannot adapt to a level in the larger life for which we are not prepared.

8. Reunion: There is a reunion with departed loved ones and friends.
There have been countless reports coming to us through credible mediumship and near-death studies indicating that we are greeted on the Other Side by deceased loved ones and that there is a happy reunion of some kind before one of those loved ones or an independent spirit takes us under his or her "wing" and guides us, explaining how things work in that realm, while also giving us a tour of the afterlife environment and then guiding us in further development there.

9. Rebirth: After the adjustment period, we settle in and spiritually evolve from there.
Whether reincarnation involves a rebirth of the total personality over many lifetimes or something much more complex in which fragments of the soul are reborn as the "higher self" remains in the spirit world in a Group Soul is unclear and apparently beyond human comprehension, but one way or the other there is a spiritual evolution taking place in which the soul learns to deal with adversity and gradually perfects itself, moving to higher and higher realms.

10. True Oneness: We retain our individuality as we spiritually evolve.
The ultimate, according to some beliefs, is the attainment of Nirvana, at which all souls become One with the Creator. While this implies a loss of individuality, various advanced spirits have informed us that it is just the opposite – we become more of an individual. We develop latent gifts, acquire greater knowledge, become stronger in character, and never lose ourselves. Complete perfection is never attained, although there is a constant striving toward it. At some point, we succeed in finding ourselves, and in the process we find greater unity with

others. "You do not lose your individuality in a sea of greater consciousness, but that depth of the ocean becomes included in your individuality," the group soul called Silver Birch explained.

The bottom line here is that by going beyond the self-imposed limits of orthodox religion and mainstream science, we can find a much more logical, more sensible, more inviting environment – one that can be reconciled with a just and loving Creator, and a Divine Plan not based on fear. At the same time, the basic tenets of the Bible and other good books – *Do unto others...*, *Love thy neighbor...*, and *You reap what you sow...*remain the guiding principles in the latest revelations.

References

Alexander, Eben, M.D., *Proof of Heaven*, Simon and Schuster, New York, 2012

Atwater, P. M. H., *A Manuel for Developing Humans*, Rainbow Ridge Books, 2017

Ballard, Stan A. & Green, Roger, The Silver Birch Book of Questions & Answers, Spiritual Truth Press, Bristol, England, 1998

Barrett, H. D., *Life Work of Cora L. V. Richmond*, InterFarFacing Publishing, 2010 (original 1895)

Barrett, Sir William, *On the Threshold of the Unseen*, E.F. Dutton & Co., New York, 1917

Barrett, Sir William Barrett, *Death-Bed Visions*, third edition, The Aquarian Press, Northamptonshire, England, 1986 (originally published in 1926)

Becker, Ernest, *The Denial of Death*, Simon & Schuster, NY, 1973

Beichler, James E., *To Die For*, Trafford Publishing, Victoria, B.C., 2008

Bellg, Laurin, M.D., *Near Death in the ICU*, Sloan Press, 2015

Berger, Arthur S. and Joyce, *The Encyclopedia of Parapsychology and Psychical Research*, Paragon House, 1991

Betty, Stafford,, *Heaven & Hell Unveiled*, White Crow Books, U. K., 2014

Betty, Stafford, *When did you ever become less by dying?* White Crow Books, U.K. 2016

Bockris, John O. M., *The New Paradigm*, New Energy Foundation, 2013

Carol, Cathi, *Skeptical about Skeptics*, Transpersonal Paradigm Publishers, 2018

Cayce, Edgar, *"No Death: God's Other Door*, A. R. E. Press, Virginia Beach, VA, 1998

Crookall, Robert, *The Supreme Adventure*, James Clarke & Co., Ltd., Cambridge, 1961

Crookall, Robert, *Out of Body Experiences*, Carol Publishing Group., New York, NY., 1970

Crookes, Sir William, *Researches into the Phenomena of Modern Spiritualism*, Austin Publishing Co., Los Angeles, Calif., 1922 (fourth edition of 1906 book)

Davis, Andrew Jackson, *Death and the After Life*, Colby and Rich, Boston, 1865

De Montaigne, Michel, *The Complete Essays*, Penguin Books, 1987

De Morgan, Sophia Elizabeth, *From Matter to Spirit*, Longman, Green Longman, Roberts & Green, London, 1863

Dostoyevsky, Fyodor, *Crime and Punishment*, Digireads.com, 2004

Doyle, Arthur Conan, *The Vital Message*, George H. Doran Company, New York, 1919

Doyle, Arthur Conan, M.D., LL.D., *The History of Spiritualism*, George H. Doran Company, New York, 1926

References

Duffey, Mrs. E. B., *Heaven Revised*, Two Worlds Publishing Co., Manchester, UK, 1921

Eddy, Sherwood, *You Will Survive Death*, The Omega Press, Surrey, England, 1954

Edmonds, John W., and Dexter, George T., *Spiritualism*, Partridge & Brittan, New York, 1853

Farr, Sidney Saylor, *What Tom Sawyer Learned from Dying*, Hampton Roads Publishing Co., Ltd., Norfolk, VA, 1993

Fenwick, Peter & Elizabeth, *The Art of Dying*, Continuum, New York, NY, 2008

Fenwick, Peter & Elizabeth, *Truth in the Light*, White Crow Books, 2012

Findlay, Arthur, *The Psychic Stream*, Psychic Press Ltd., London, 1939

Flammarion, Camille, *Death and Its Mystery: Before Death*, T. Fisher Unwin, Ltd., London, 1922

Ford, Sarah Louise, *Interwoven*, The Progressive Thinker Publishing House, Chicago, 1907

Frankl, Viktor F., *Man's Search for Meaning*, Washington Square Press, NY, 1984

Garland, Hamlin, *Forty Years of Psychic Research*, The MacMillan Co., New York, 1936

Garrett, Eileen J. *Awareness*, Creative Age Press, Inc., New York, NY, 1943

Gilbert, Alice, *Philip in the Spheres*, The Aquarian Press, London, 1952

Greaves, Helen, *The Challenging Light*, Neville Spearman, Suffolk, UK, 1984

Greber, Johannes, *Communication with The Spirit World of God*, Johannes Greber Memorial Foundation, Teaneck, NJ, 1979

Greyson, Bruce, M.D., *After!* St. Martin's Essentials, 20121

Hampton, Charles, Transition, St. Albans Press, Los Angeles, 1943 (1911 NDE)

Harding, Emma, *Modern American Spiritualism*, University Books, New Hyde Park, NY, 1970 (reprint of 1869 book)

Hare, Robert, M.D., *Experimental Investigation of the Spirit Manifestations*, Partridge & Brittan, New York, 1855

Hart, Roger, *The Phaselock Code*, Paraview, New York, 2003

Heagerty, N. Riley, *The French Revelation*, Morris Publishing, 2000

Hegy, Reginald, *A Witness Through the Centuries*, E. P. Dutton & Co., Inc. New York, NY, 1935

Holt, Henry, *On the Cosmic Relations*, Houghton Mifflin Company, Boston and New York, 1914

Hogan, R. Craig, Ph.D., *Your Eternal Self*, Greater Reality Publications, 2020

Hugenot, Alan Ross, *The Death Experience*, Hugenot Books, 2023

Hugenot, Alan Ross, *The New Science of Consciousness Survival*, Hugenot Books, 2023

Hyslop, James H., *Contact with the Other World*, The Century Co., New York, 1919

James, William, *The Varieties of Religious Experience*, 1902

Jung, C. G., *Memories, Dreams, Reflections*, Vintage Books, NY, 1961

Jung, C. G., *Modern Man in Search of a Soul*, Harcourt Brace Jovanovich Publishers, 1933

Kardec, Allan, *The Spirits' Book*, Amapse Society, Mexico, reprint from 1857

References

Kierkegaard, S., *Fear and Trembling*, Doubleday & Co., Garden City, NY, 1954

Kubler-Ross, Elisabeth, *On Life After Death*, Celestial Arts, Berkeley, Calif.

Leonard, Gladys Osborne, *The Last Crossing*, Psychic Book Club, London, 1937

Lodge, Oliver, *The Survival of Man*, Moffat, Yard and Co., New York, 1909

Lodge, Oliver, *Past Years*, Charles Scribner's Sons, New York, 1932

Long, Jefferey with Perry, *Paul, Evidence of the Afterlife*, Harper Collins Publishers, New York, NY, 2010

Mack, John E. M.D., *Passport to the Cosmos*, White Crow Books, UK, 2011

Medhurst, R. G., *Crookes and the Spirit World*, Taplinger Publishing Co., New York, NY 1972

Moody, Raymond, *Glimpses of Eternity*, Guideposts, New York, NY, 2010

Moody, Raymond, *Life After Life*, Mockingbird Books, 1976

Morse, Melvin, M.D. (with Paul Perry), *Parting Visions*, Villard Books, New York, 1994

Moses, William Stainton, *More Spirit Teachings*, Meilach.com

Myers, F. W. H., *Human Personality and its Survival of Bodily Death*, University Books, Inc., New Hyde Park, NY, 1961 (reprint of 1903 book)

Osis, Karlis and Haraldsson, Erlendur, *At the Hour of Death*, Avon Books, New York, 1977

Owen, G. Vale, *The Life Beyond The Veil*, George H. Doran Co., New York, 1921

Paget, Fanny Ruthven, *How I Know That the Dear are Alive*, Plenty Publishing Co., Washington, D.C., 1917

Ring, Kenneth & Cooper, Sharon, *Mindsight*, William James Center for Consciousness Studies, 1999

Rinpoche, Sogyal, *The Tibetan Book of Living and Dying*, Harper, San Francisco,1994

Sabom, Michael B., *Light & Death*, Zondervan Publishing House, Grand Rapids, Michigan, 1998

Schmicker, Michael, *Best Evidence*, iuniverse, 2002

Scott, John, *As One Ghost to Another*, Spiritualist Press Ltd., London, 1948

Sculthorp, Frederick C., *Excursions to the Spirit World*, The Greater World Assoc., London, 1961

Sheldrake, Rupert, *Science Set Free*, Deepak Chopra Books, New York, 2012

Schwartz, Gary E., Ph.D., *The Afterlife Experiments*, Pocket Books, New York, N.Y., 2002

Schwartz, Gary E., Ph.D., *The Sacred Promise*, Atria Books & Beyond Words, 2011

Swedenborg, Emanuel, *Heaven & Hell*, Swedenborg Foundation, West Chester, PA, 1976

Thomas, Charles Drayton, *Life Beyond Death with Evidence*, W. Collins Sons. & Co., Glasgow, 1928

Thomas, Charles Drayton, *Some New Evidence for Human Survival*, Spiritualist Press Ltd., London, 1922, (Revised 1948, no copyright)

Vandenbush, Bill, *If Morning Never Comes*, White Crow Books, 2016

Van Lommel, Pim, M.D., *Consciousness Beyond Life*, Harper Collins Publishers, 2010

References

Wallace, Alfred Russel, *Miracles and Modern Spiritualism*, George Redway, London, 1896

White, Steward Edward, *Across the Unknown*, Ariel Press, Columbus, OH, 1987

White, Stewart Edward, *The Unobstructed Universe*, E. P. Dutton & Co., New York, 1940

Whiting, Lilian, *The Spiritual Significance*, Little, Brown, & Co., Boston, 1901

Zammit, Victor, *A Lawyer Presents the Case for the Afterlife*, White Crow Books, UK, 2012

About the Author

～

A 1958 graduate of the San Jose State College School of Journalism and a current resident of Kailua, Hawaii, Michael Tymn spent three years as an officer in the United States Marine Corps and 40 years in insurance claims adjusting, supervision and management before retirement in 2002. He has been a freelance journalist for more than 70 years, having contributed some 2,000 articles, columns, and essays to 50 or more publications. Writing assignments and projects, covering business, sports, travel, historical, and metaphysical subjects, have taken him to such diverse places as Jerusalem, Hollywood, Bangkok, Panama, St. Paul, Tombstone, Glastonbury, and Kona. He has authored seven other books, including *The Afterlife Revealed, Resurrecting Leonora Piper,* and *No One Really Dies* and has received awards for his essays in contests sponsored by the American Public Relations Association (1960), The Academy for Spirituality & Consciousness Studies (1999) and the Bigelow Institute for Consciousness Studies (2021). He was one of the first inductees to the Hawaii Running Hall of Fame, honored for both his writing contributions to the sport and his competitive victories.

www.ingramcontent.com/pod-product-compliance
Lightning Source LLC
Chambersburg PA
CBHW030835090426
42737CB00009B/978